Hammered Flowers

HERBERT PRESS
Bloomsbury Publishing Plc
50 Bedford Square, London, WC1B 3DP, UK
Bloomsbury Publishing Ireland Limited, 29 Earlsfort Terrace, Dublin 2, D02 AY28, Ireland

BLOOMSBURY, HERBERT PRESS and the Herbert Press logo are trademarks of Bloomsbury Publishing Plc

First published in Great Britain 2026

Copyright © Michelle Moore, 2026

Michelle Moore has asserted her right under the Copyright, Designs and Patents Act, 1988, to be identified as Author of this work

All rights reserved. No part of this publication may be: i) reproduced or transmitted in any form, electronic or mechanical, including photocopying, recording or by means of any information storage or retrieval system without prior permission in writing from the publishers; or ii) used or reproduced in any way for the training, development or operation of artificial intelligence (AI) technologies, including generative AI technologies. The rights holders expressly reserve this publication from the text and data mining exception as per Article 4(3) of the Digital Single Market Directive (EU) 2019/790

Bloomsbury Publishing Plc does not have any control over, or responsibility for, any third-party websites referred to or in this book. All internet addresses given in this book were correct at the time of going to press. The author and publisher regret any inconvenience caused if addresses have changed or sites have ceased to exist, but can accept no responsibility for any such changes

A catalogue record for this book is available from the British Library

Library of Congress Cataloguing-in-Publication data has been applied for

ISBN: PB: 9781789943184; eBook: 9781789943177

2 4 6 8 10 9 7 5 3 1

Design by Laura Woussen
Typeset in Josefin Sans by Santiago Orozco and Fiora Monograms by Crystal Kluge
Printed and bound in China by RR Donnelley Asia Printing Solutions Limited

To find out more about our authors and books visit www.bloomsbury.com and sign up for our newsletters

For product safety related questions contact productsafety@bloomsbury.com

For Mom, Dad, and all those who have unconditionally supported my endless journey in the arts.

To my furry loves, Freyja, Raven, and Nova, who allowed me to scratch their sweet little heads while I wrote this book.

And the Captain, who helps me make all of my biggest dreams a reality. I love you.

Lastly, to the creatives of the world... Just keep hammering away a little at a time.

PAGE 1 *image: A traditional ball-peen hammer is surrounded by homegrown flowers that can be used to create color on fabric.*

PAGE 3 *image: Flower hammering in progress for a floral fabric shoe project (see pages 130–31).*

MICHELLE MOORE

Hammered Flowers

Printing on fabric, paper and wood

HERBERT PRESS
LONDON · OXFORD · NEW YORK · NEW DELHI · SYDNEY

CONTENTS

INTRODUCTION — 8

PART ONE: GETTING STARTED — 10

Sourcing the best botanicals for printing — 12
  Growing your own natural dye garden — 12
  Foraging in your natural environment — 20
  Purchasing plants and flowers — 24
  Locally sourcing flower waste — 25

Tools and materials — 28
  Basic supplies — 28
  Choosing your project material — 31

Preparation and hammering — 34
  Working with natural dyes and mordants — 34
  Preparing flowers and leaves for hammering — 35
  The hammering technique — 36

Scouring, mordanting, and using modifiers — 38
  Scouring fabric — 38
  Mordanting fabric — 41
  Using modifiers — 53

Washing and aftercare — 58

PART TWO: THE PROJECTS — 60

Projects on fabric — 62
  Treasure pouches — 64
  Garment patches — 68
  Hand-torn ribbons — 72
  Cosmos garden socks — 76
  Black hollyhock butterfly bandanna — 80
  Summer striped linen blouse — 85
  Velvet flower scarf — 88
  Japanese indigo table runner — 90
  Tomato tea towel — 96

OPPOSITE *Flowers are arranged in small groups for ease of selection when hammering.*

Projects on paper and wood — 100
    Flowery gift tags — 103
    Botanical bookmarks — 106
    Bouquet greeting card — 110
    Decoupage flower journal — 114
    Wildflower wooden coasters — 118

Inspirational pieces — 122
    Viola and pansy tote bag — 125
    Vintage boho dress — 128
    Floral fabric — 130
    Wildflower garden apron — 132
    Vintage table runner — 134

Finishing touches — 136
    Stencils — 138
    Resists — 139
    Artwork — 142
    Digitizing your work — 146
    Embroidery — 147
    Paper punches — 148

Practice pages — 150
    Hand holding flowers — 152
    Peace wreath — 153
    On the windowsill — 154

GLOSSARY — 155

RESOURCES — 158

OPPOSITE *Experimenting with composition and placement before hammering flowers onto the potted design.*

INTRODUCTION

I remember the first time I tried flower hammering; the results were messy and indistinguishable. After a lot of practice with different flowers and approaches, I arrived at my first "perfect print" and I was instantly hooked.

I was so intrigued that it was possible to transfer color and shape from a flower so it looked as though it had been digitally printed on the surface of the fabric. That spark led to more and more experimentation and ultimately the creation of all of the projects and explorations found within the pages of this book.

I hope that it brings you joy to discover this enchanting art form, filled with curiosity and potential that is only limited by your own imagination.

Happy hammering,

Flowers hammered onto cotton canvas to create a unique and vibrant wall hanging.

WHAT IS FLOWER AND LEAF HAMMERING?

Flower and leaf hammering is the art of transferring colors and shapes from botanical matter onto fabric and paper. This beautiful art form involves using a hammer, mallet, or even a smooth rock to pound the color from the botanical matter onto the surface. This process, also called Tataki-zomé (hammering dye), is a traditional Japanese technique that has been used for hundreds (possibly thousands) of years.

To print successfully, you must identify flowers and leaves that are good for this process and understand why. While most plants will work for this process, I will share with you some of my favorite leaves and flowers (see pages 16-19) for creating "perfect" prints, time and time again.

Some flowers will leave beautiful prints but will not have good color retention, meaning the dye will not stay on the fabric for long. Others will have better natural dye properties, which will make them a great choice for flower hammering.

So, get ready, clear your workspace, and let's dive into the charming world of flower and leaf hammering!

PART ONE
GETTING STARTED

SOURCING THE BEST BOTANICALS FOR PRINTING

Plants for printing can be sourced in a number of ways: you can grow your own, forage in your natural environment, purchase them, or even locally source flower waste from events or pick-your-own flower growers. I highly recommend that you explore and experiment with your local environment as much as possible, as nature will have a way of surprising you. Observation is the key to success with this technique. Take notes and pay close attention to which plants are giving you beautiful colors and shapes. Notice the details. Be curious.

GROWING YOUR OWN NATURAL DYE GARDEN

A selection of cosmos and coreopsis flowers, picked and ready to be hammered onto fabric and paper.

Growing your own flowers and leaves is a great way to ensure that you will get the quantity and quality of plants that you most enjoy working with. A dye garden can be as big or small as you desire or have space for. When I started, I became overwhelmed by all of the varieties available, but the reality is, you can work with just about any flower once you understand the technique.

You will need to decide whether you care how long your prints will last. If you are creating a quick gift tag, it may be okay for your prints to have a shorter lifespan. If you are selling or gifting an item, you may want to pretreat or mordant it (see pages 41–52) so the prints last longer. Select flowers and leaves with good natural dye properties before you begin to ensure maximum color- and lightfastness.

In my own garden, I have a few "must-grow" plants that are known for their great natural dye properties and also make fabulous hammered flower prints. Cosmos and coreopsis are available in many varieties, shapes, colors, and sizes. Japanese indigo leaves are a must, as are Blacknight hollyhocks for the dark rich blue-purple hues they leave behind.

The first Blacknight hollyhock of the season blooms.

You can consider a simple dye garden consisting of a few pots with easy-to-grow wildflowers. You can also use raised or non-traditional garden beds. For example, I use a raised watering trough from my local hardware store for my Japanese indigo bed, which keeps them contained and easy to care for, maintain, and harvest.

Consider utilizing a local community garden, look for starter plants or plugs at local garden centers, or ask smaller nurseries to carry a specific plant you are interested in growing. Or why not reach out to a neighbor, friend, family member, or local farm to see if you can plant flowers on their land? You will be surprised how many people welcome this idea or are already growing flowers that are perfect for this process. Get creative!

I created a natural dye garden at my parents' home to increase the yield of my seasonal flower harvest. I first tilled the soil and then added fresh nutrient-rich compost on top. I then added small rocks to the walkways and a weed mat to help control unwanted growth. Next, I planted rows of my favorite natural dye flowers.

A Japanese indigo (Persicaria tinctoria) seedling—grown from seed in a plantable, eco-friendly container—emerges from the soil. Burlap and an indigo-dyed ribbon are wrapped around the pot, making it suitable for gifting.

Japanese indigo plants, grown in a raised watering trough.

My newly planted natural dye garden, ready for the growing season. Here I am growing (left to right) Black Hopi sunflowers, Sulfur cosmos, Black hollyhocks, Black Knight scabiosa, marigolds, and coreopsis.

FAVORITE FLOWERS AND LEAVES FOR HAMMERING

The following are some of my favorite flowers, plants, leaves, and petals to hammer, not due to their fastness but because of the way they print on fabric and paper. Be sure to identify any unknown plants before working with them, and discard hammered materials away from children and pets.

Flowers
- Bachelor's Buttons (cornflower)
- Bidens
- Black-eyed Susan petals
- Cosmos
- Coreopsis
- Flowering herb plants (e.g. dill, basil, chamomile)
- Goldenrod
- Hollyhocks: Blacknight or Burgundy
- Marigold petals
- Rose petals
- Viola and pansy varieties

Leaves
- Birch
- Black walnut
- Coleus
- Cosmos foliage
- Coreopsis foliage
- Ferns
- Goldenrod
- Herbs: sage, parsley, dill, basil
- Japanese indigo and other indigo-bearing leaves
- Mimosa/Albizia
- Nasturtiums
- Smoke bush
- Staghorn sumac
- Tansy and yarrow leaves
- Tomato leaves
- Weld/Dyer's rocket

There are some flowers and leaves that may appear as though they would work well for this process but due to their inherent moisture content do not. For example, zinnias, which come in lots of bright, beautiful colors, do not print well due to a lower moisture content in their petals. Also, hydrangeas, lavender, celosia, all dried flowers, flowers nearing the end of their lives, and pressed flowers will not work. You need the botanicals to have some but not too much water in them for good pigment transfer.

Violas and pansies.

RIGHT Over the years, I have sourced and grown many varieties of coreopsis and cosmos flowers because they vary so much in color and shape. Here are just a few of my favorites.

SOURCING THE BEST BOTANICALS FOR PRINTING

FLOWERS AND PLANTS TO AVOID

The following flowers and plants should not be hammered as they contain known toxins, which may be harmful if touched while hammering is in progress or afterward. Please proceed with caution with any unknown plant you may come in contact with, and make sure to properly identify it before continuing – you definitely don't want to hammer a poisonous leaf or flower!

Do Not Hammer
- Any poison plant (ivy, sumac, oak)
- Foxgloves
- Hogweed
- Latana
- Lily of the valley
- Oleander
- Water hemlock

The best way to figure out what works best is to try new plants and see what kinds of prints you can achieve. It has become increasingly easy to identify flowers with the use of your smartphone and plant identification apps. You can also pick up wildflower field guides for your specific region for when you are foraging. I am a big fan of collecting vintage field guides from all over the world.

COSMOS AND COREOPSIS

Cosmos and coreopsis flowers are available in more than 40 varieties that are suitable for a natural dye garden. These flowers are known for their abundant blooming, allowing for continuous picking without hindering their growth. Most cosmos varieties are resilient and will flower throughout the season, thriving in various soil conditions and preferring ample sunlight. They can be cultivated in pots on porches, as garden borders, or in raised beds, attracting numerous pollinators to the garden. While cosmos are annuals, they can self-seed if left to grow naturally, particularly the Sulfur variety, which has reliably reseeded itself for years. In contrast, coreopsis are perennials that return each season.

TOP LEFT *Different varieties of homegrown coreopsis or tickseed plants. Great for hammering, these perennials will come back each season.*

TOP RIGHT *A bouquet of freshy picked Sulfur cosmos flowers in a beautiful, vibrant orange.*

BOTTOM LEFT *A variety of pink and purple cosmos flowers.*

BOTTOM RIGHT *Lil' Bang coreopsis flowers.*

FORAGING IN YOUR NATURAL ENVIRONMENT

Take a walk, see what you can find, and experiment with local wildflowers, leaves, and ferns. You can bring a lightweight rubber mallet or use a smooth rock on your adventures to make a print. Even if a flower looks like it wouldn't work, give it a try and see what happens. Making prints as you go can be a good way to document your local botanicals and bring home a sweet souvenir from your summer trek.

PAGE 22 *The leaves and flowers from a mimosa tree (also known as an albizia or Persian silk tree) were a pleasant surprise. They were hammered on to mordanted cloth to test their color potential. Even the fluffy flowers and buds left beautiful marks on the fabric.*

ABOVE *Gathering sunchoke flowers on a summer hike in the mountains.*

ABOVE RIGHT *An albizia tree in full bloom.*

RIGHT *Summer ferns hammered on a hike by a waterfall.*

PAGE 23 *Cornflowers (also known as Bachelor's Buttons) are wildflowers that can be found in a variety of colors. High in pigment, they make great prints – especially when hammered on their side to create a "fan." These Black Magic Bachelor's Buttons are high in anthocyanin pigment. Their color will shift easily with the use of a modifier (see pages 53-57).*

PURCHASING PLANTS AND FLOWERS

Purchasing plants and flowers is a great way to keep experimenting and seeing what kinds of colors and shapes are possible in any season. In the offseason, when freshly picked flowers aren't readily available, you can purchase flowers from grocery stores or florists. Keep in mind that store-bought flowers can sometimes contain artificial color or pigment that may transfer onto your project.

Garden centers often have houseplants and potted herbs that can be fun to experiment with. Sage, basil, mint, and parsley work well, giving beautiful clean prints that vary in fastness but are great to practice with.

Rose petals are great for cutting shapes from their leaves to hammer onto surfaces. Their anthocyanin pigment allows them to be modified to create a range of interesting colors. They can also be hammered as a whole flower to form a lovely rose-flower print.

Store-bought flowers provide a range of colors in the offseason.

Leftover red roses from a Valentine's Day bouquet.

LOCALLY SOURCING FLOWER WASTE

It's amazing how waste can be turned into something beautiful and useful if we go looking for it. You can locally source flower waste from a number of different places. Events such as weddings and parties often have lots of floral waste. You can also check with event planners by sending a friendly message via Instagram or email to discover where their discarded flowers will end up. You might find you make a connection that will continue to provide you with a source of free botanicals on a regular basis.

I reached out to my local hemp farm, Hepworth Farms, and they allowed me to use their leaf trimmings to create prints with. The leaves could also be used to create a dye bath for an all-over brilliant-yellow dye. I held leaf-hammering workshops at their store and promoted their business, so that it was mutually beneficial. These relationships can become a great source of plants for natural dyes and experimentation.

While we might not all have hemp farms locally, consider what is abundant in your own environment. I encourage creating relationships with your local community. Everything big starts small.

A large hemp leaf hammered onto a cotton bandanna.

A handful of freshly picked hemp leaves.

I am also grateful to have access to several incredible 'pick-your-own' flower farms in my region. They are a great source of inspiration and provide a variety of flowers I don't typically grow, to practice and experiment with. They often till over the land at the end of the season, so you may be able to ask to harvest the end-of-season crop to use for your craft.

Research your area and see if this type of farm exists near you. If not, reach out and start a conversation with someone who might be able to help. I have found that most people are quite generous when it comes to flowers. They are a beautiful universal language that we all can appreciate.

Pick-your-own flowers at Brittany Hollow Farm, Rhinebeck, New York.

TOOLS AND MATERIALS

In general, hammering flowers and leaves does not require much equipment. In its simplest form, you will need something to hammer with, plants, a cover cloth, and the item that you will be embellishing or designing.

Once you start to make progress on more defined prints, you will want to consider the type of fabric or paper you are hammering onto, the surface on which you are hammering, and the type of hammer or mallet you are using. You will also need to decide if you are going to mordant your fabric or paper for longer-lasting prints (see pages 41–52).

There are many variables when working this way that will yield lots of different outcomes. Once you start to practice, you will become increasingly aware of how each of these elements plays an important role in the printing process.

BASIC SUPPLIES

The following items become very important when you are working toward creating precise prints that have clear petal definition and leaf veining.

Tools required
- Regular hammers or rubber mallets
- Cover cloth – any natural-fiber material
- Wooden flat surface or cutting board
- Flowers and leaves
- Prepared project material or paper
- Rubber gloves
- Scissors
- Dust mask

Mordant supplies, if pretreating your work
- Kitchen scale
- Measuring spoons
- Synthrapol for scouring fabric
- Alum (potassium alum sulfate or alum acetate)
- Soda ash
- Designated natural dye equipment (e.g. pots, stir spoons)
- Tannin (e.g. tea, sumac, oak gall, or tara)

HAMMERS VS. RUBBER MALLETS

Both hammers and rubber mallets will work effectively. However, when an artist paints a landscape, do they use one brush? Just as an artist has many tools, it is good to have a selection of mallets and hammers available while you are working, and as you learn and practice, you'll develop an understanding of which hammer or mallet works best for the specific botanical you are working with. I often switch out my hammer for a mallet or vice versa to get the clearest prints. This is especially important when working on a project that has many varieties of flowers and leaves.

Rubber mallets come in a variety of sizes and weights but generally have a much larger surface area than a regular hammer, which helps to make cleaner prints. I tend to stick to the lighter-weight mallets that are under 16 oz (450 g), which are easier to work with for larger projects as your arm doesn't get tired as quickly. It is better to err on the side of less force than too much, so you don't completely obliterate the plant, leaving a mess rather than the flower print. If I had to pick just one tool to do this process with it would be a lightweight rubber mallet.

Hammers tend to have a smaller surface area and more weight than rubber mallets, and therefore can create more force. This can result in unwanted marks at the edge of the print, where the hammer meets the fabric, often resulting in a pressure line or mark that will create texture or variation which you may not desire in your project. Hammers that you would normally use for nails are great for leaves or flowers that are tough and bulky. Think about the difference between a tree leaf like an oak or maple, and a delicate flower petal – while the hammer will work for both plants, the hammer is better for the tree leaf and the rubber mallet for the delicate flower.

OTHER HAMMERING TOOLS

As well as hammers and mallets, you can also find smooth river rocks, spoons, or wooden blocks to use as hammering devices. While these aren't always the best choice for "perfect prints," they will leave color and are a lot of fun for experimentation. As you gain experience, you will start to understand what the best tool for the project you are working on is. I like to have a variety on hand so that I can pick and choose as needed.

Rubber mallets and a traditional metal hammer.

Seafood mallets

If you are working with children, you might want to consider some lighter options like wooden seafood mallets. These tend to be lightweight and are easier to use.

Texture hammers

Additionally, there are craft hammers that come with interchangeable textured surfaces that will allow you to create a variety of marks and patterns on fabric or paper. Traditionally used for jewelry making, these hammers can be great for creating backgrounds or adding more interest to a piece. I have seen lots of different options, from dots to waves and lines.

Try laying down lots of different petals and hammering with a texture hammer to see what kind of patterns you can achieve.

LEFT *Here flower petals were individually removed and hammered onto the surface of the paper to create a mandala. The final step was to add pattern using a texture hammer.*

CHOOSING YOUR PROJECT MATERIAL

FABRIC TYPES

First and foremost, natural dyes do best when paired with natural fibers, meaning you can choose either plant fibers, such as bamboo, cotton, flax, hemp, or ramie, or animal fibers, such as alpaca, angora, silk, or wool, for your projects. I work mostly with silk from the animal fiber category; however, I have hammered flowers on wool with good results. There are also man-made regenerated fibers that are derived from renewable raw materials, such as lyocell, modal, and rayon, making them a good choice for natural dye.

You can also find blends of the above fibers, for example cotton/hemp or silk/cotton. Be careful not to choose a fabric that has a high synthetic fiber content, although fabrics with a small amount (5%) of spandex or stretch can often increase the desirability of your prints.

Avoid synthetic materials, such as polyester, acrylic, and nylon. There are cases where you may want to experiment with these fabrics, but I suggest starting with natural fibers first as they will give you a better affinity for natural dyes in the bigger picture.

The weave of your fabric is another important detail. Fabric that has a tighter weave with more threads per square inch can create a much clearer, crisper print. If you work on a looser weave, with fewer threads per square inch, the print may be significantly less detailed.

The fabric you choose will depend on your desired outcome and the final use of the project you create. I strongly encourage experimentation with different materials, as you never know what outcome will interest you most. Fabrics that I favor for flower and leaf hammering include cotton and silk.

Cotton canvas stands out as one of the first materials I utilized to achieve sharp and pristine prints, making it highly recommended for experimentation. It is readily available by the yard in various weights at art and craft supply shops. Additionally, cotton muslin, jersey, and t-shirts are easily sourced, upcycled, and purchased, making them excellent choices for practice and experimentation. Check the fiber content to ensure a predominance of natural fibers, with a small allowance for synthetics. A hemp/cotton blend also proves to be an outstanding option.

Silk is particularly effective in this process due to its remarkable color retention. I enjoy printing on silk ribbons, pillowcases, and thrifted blouses. Lastly, silk velvet is an exceptional and surprising fabric for flower and leaf hammering, producing beautiful, luxurious results that are worth exploring.

PAPER TYPES

Various types of paper are suitable for flower and leaf hammering, each offering unique characteristics.

- Mulberry paper – derived from the bark of the mulberry tree – appears delicate, yet possesses long fiber strands that enhance its durability, making it ideal for decoupage.

- Watercolor paper, available in hot press and cold press varieties, is heavier and more absorbent, effectively retaining water and pigment without blurring; hot press is preferred for its smooth surface.

- Card stock – thicker and more robust than standard paper – serves as an economical choice for experimentation and performs well in both mordanting and hammering, making it suitable for bookmarks and gift tags.

- Mixed-media paper combines the qualities of watercolor and drawing paper, providing a versatile option that withstands moisture while maintaining a durable surface.

- Tissue paper, although delicate, can yield clear prints without being mordanted. It is excellent for adding a special touch to a hammered flower gift.

- Lastly, handmade paper offers diverse results based on its texture.

COVER CLOTHS

A cover cloth is a material that is used to do just that... cover! I like to use cotton for this. I use this piece of fabric over the top of the flower or leaf that I am hammering, and it allows excess moisture and pigment to absorb somewhere other than the project. Without the cover cloth, you run this risk of oversaturation and therefore messy, less desirable prints. Hammering directly on to the botanical will rarely, if ever, give you a clear flower or leaf print.

A cover cloth is used on a cosmos flower, resulting in a floral print on both the project fabric and the cover cloth.

You can choose to have your cover cloth mordanted or not. I usually use untreated fabric as I don't want to "waste" my pretreated fabric. However, if you plan accordingly, you can create two pieces at once by designing your cover piece at the same time as your project, as most leaves and flowers will give two unique prints. I also like laundering my unmordanted cover cloth to see which pigments had the best color retention without the use of a mordant. It becomes a side experiment to my projects.

Wooden picnic tables also work well, but you need to be mindful of the grooves between the boards as they will show up in your project if you don't have good placement of your botanicals. Wooden workbenches are a perfect surface to hammer onto as well.

Thicker plastic boards can work as well; however, they often have a textured surface. If you have a plastic board, you can lay down a cloth first before placing your project.

Surfaces with texture, imperfections, or that are bumpy or uneven are poor options. Those imperfections will show up in your project or cause you to miss a spot when you are hammering. However, the addition of texture from the surface you are hammering onto may be a desirable effect at some point, so keep playing to discover what is possible.

Cover cloth from hammering Japanese indigo leaves. This became a beautiful piece without planning or mordanting this fabric.

I have also seen the use of plastic as a cover. I have found that it causes splatter and pigment bleed, resulting in less-than-perfect prints. The plastic tends to act as a resist, causing the pigment to bounce back onto the project. However, I think that this would be a good option when working with children, as they will be able to see what they are doing better while they are hammering.

HAMMERING SURFACES

The surface on which you hammer and create your project is important. You want a surface that has "give," not one that is too hard or uneven. The best surface that I have found for printing is wooden cutting boards placed on top of a sturdy surface. They are smooth and have just enough "give" to enable beautiful hammered prints. Having a variety of surfaces or cutting boards readily available is helpful. Often, a smaller, more portable surface is nice to have on hand. Small cutting boards are good for hammering little projects like gift tags, bookmarks, or details on a shirt sleeve. I source all of my cutting boards from thrift shops. The great thing is, if the surface has wear, dirt, or debris, you can sand it to make it as good as new.

A variety of cutting boards used as my project surfaces for hammering botanicals.

PREPARATION AND HAMMERING

In order to have the best possible outcomes when working with hammered flowers and leaves, there are a few factors you should consider before making a start. First, you need to source your supplies and organize your work station; then you will need to gather your botanicals; and, lastly, you will need to practice your hammering technique. If you consider all of these factors in advance, you will set yourself up for a successful hammering session with optimum results.

WORKING WITH NATURAL DYES AND MORDANTS

Although we are working with natural elements, natural does not always mean "non-toxic." Always identify any unfamiliar plant you are working with and its toxicity level before you begin. Keep your natural dye materials separate from your regular kitchen equipment to avoid possible food contamination or ingestion of a foreign substance. Wearing gloves is also a good idea when working with an unknown plant, especially if you have sensitive skin. Plants that you do not identify first run the risk of causing skin irritations or rashes.

I have sourced many of my natural dye supplies from local thrift stores, yard sales, and even online marketplaces. Be on the lookout for cutting boards, large stainless-steel pots that you can use to mordant fabrics, roasting pans for mordanting paper, measuring spoons and cups, and drying racks. You can also look for different kinds of hammers and mallets to add to your collection.

Keep your work area clean and organized so that you do not contaminate your project. Once fabric and paper are mordanted, they will be extremely susceptible to stains and accidental dyeing. It is best to put fabric in a storage container, out of direct sunlight, until you are ready to use it. A tidy environment to create in, with all of your tools readily available, will give you better outcomes and more room for creativity to bloom.

PREPARING FLOWERS AND LEAVES FOR HAMMERING

When you start to experiment with flowers and leaves for hammering, there are a few things to keep in mind. Pay attention to the feel of the leaf. Does it feel waxy or leathery? These are not good options for hammering as the surfaces will not allow for easy transfer of pigment. Look for leaves and petals that feel soft, thin, and smooth.

Pay attention to the time of day you pick your flowers and leaves and the kinds of prints that they leave behind — this can be an important detail when hammering your botanicals. Consider the amount of moisture that is present, both inside and outside the plant matter. If you pick flowers and leaves in the early morning, they may be covered in dew; if you pick flowers later in the day after the hot sun has been beating on them, they may have less water retention than usual. I prefer to pick flowers in the morning. If they are slightly damp, I just dry them on a towel before I hammer them. Too much water will cause bleeding, and not enough will create a spotty print — it is a delicate balance between the two to achieve the perfect print.

When flowers have a lot of layered petals, strip some away first to minimize the chance of a blurry print. There are also flowers that you think would work great but find they don't leave much color at all, such as zinnias. Other flowers work best if you simply remove the petals and hammer them individually. This can be great for creating mandalas or designing specific patterns on your cloth, for example a stripe or plaid.

The petals from a Burning Ember marigold (above) are removed and hammered, sun-side down, one at a time, to create a design on the fabric (left). This takes advantage of the inherent pattern on the petals; a great way to add interest to a project.

A mandala is hammered onto the fabric using both whole flowers and individually removed petals from Black-eyed Susans, marigolds, cosmos, and coreopsis flowers.

THE HAMMERING TECHNIQUE

It is a good idea to have a "test cloth" or a piece of fabric on hand to test which side of the petal or leaf prints "best." On the test cloth, experiment with using a rubber mallet as well as a regular hammer to decide which will give optimum results for that plant. If you figure this out in advance, you can proceed to your project with more confidence of how the botanical will print and achieve your desired outcome more easily.

Once you have placed your flower or leaf on the hammering surface, lay your cover cloth over the top of the botanical. Make sure the cloth is nice and flat, with no wrinkles, when laying it down. Sometimes an extra cloth on the hammering surface is needed to create a place for additional moisture absorption. This can be helpful when hammering less-absorbent surfaces, such as paper, or more delicate fabrics, such as silk.

Next, choose a regular hammer or rubber mallet. If you are hammering a flower, start by lightly tapping the center to "tack it" in place, then begin at the top and hammer in a clockwise motion with even pressure. Gently peel back the cover cloth occasionally to make sure you don't miss a spot. You will be able to tell the hammered petal from the non-hammered petal by its color and adherence to the project material; petals generally turn translucent or darken when hammered. Make sure the entire petal is stuck to the cloth. If it is not, replace the cover, and hammer in that specific spot. Once you are sure the flower has been successfully hammered, gently peel or pick the petals off the surface. If you wipe the petals away too hard, you will risk the pigment moving onto the area around the prints and staining the fabric.

Follow the same process for leaves, but choose a starting point and then work from left to right or top to bottom, being sure to hammer the entire surface. Use a regular hammer for leaves as they can be a bit tougher and need more pressure. They will also have a side that will print better, depending on the foliage, and you can incorporate this into your project if you plan ahead. However, all plants and flowers will give you two interesting prints.

Pro Tip
For larger projects, keep flowers fresh while you are working by floating their heads in a shallow bowl of water. Be sure to pat them dry before use. This will prevent them from drying out or shriveling before you are ready to use them. It also helps you to clearly see which flowers you have available for printing, so you can make better, more thoughtful compositions.

RIGHT *Keeping flowers fresh in a bowl of water.*

SCOURING, MORDANTING, AND USING MODIFIERS

Scouring, mordanting, and using modifiers will enhance your hammered printing projects, by enabling better uptake and bonding of pigment and providing the opportunity to play with color.

Put simply, scouring is the removal of manufacturing chemicals, waxes, dirt, and debris that find their way onto your fabric. By removing these elements, you will allow for more even uptake of the pigment into the fiber and increased vibrancy of color. When working with natural dyes, scouring is one of the most important steps to creating work that has vibrant colors and lasting, durable prints.

Mordanting is how we bond pigment to fiber. When you mordant your fabric or paper, you are creating a place for the natural pigment found in the botanicals to adhere to. Without this important step, colors will look dull, turn brown, and fade soon after washing. There are many ways to approach mordanting your fabric. I am going to teach you three different methods: one for plant fibers, another for animal fibers, and a third way that uses soy milk in place of a metal salt.

Modifiers change the original color of the petals to give a broad spectrum of hues from one single flower. You can use natural household ingredients, such as lemon juice and baking soda, to make the color more acidic or basic, causing a shift in hue.

SCOURING FABRIC

Scouring differs from simply washing the fabric as it is more abrasive and will properly prepare the fiber for natural dye. Of course, if you would simply like to get to the fun part — hammering flowers — then go for it! This step is most important when working on a project that you want to have long-lasting prints.

To scour your fabric, you must consider the type of fabric you are working with as well as the weight of fiber (WOF). Even brand-new fabric needs to be scoured. You can scour your plant/cellulose fabric in two different ways:

1 In a washing machine

2 In a pot, large enough to hold your fabric so that it can move freely on a heat source.

I generally scour all my fabric in the washing machine, as I have found it to be simple and effective, especially when working with yardage or bigger pieces of clothing. Both cellulose scour and synthrapol are similar in their ability to remove impurities from fiber prior to dyeing. While cellulose scour is better suited for plant-based fibers, you can use synthrapol on plant- and animal-based fibers when used in conjunction with soda ash. You can source this through any online natural dye supplier or even at art supply stores.

SCOURING PLANT/CELLULOSE FABRIC USING A WASHING MACHINE

You will need
- Dry fabric
- Kitchen scale
- Soda ash
- Cellulose scour or synthrapol
- Washing machine

1. Weigh the dry fabric.

2. Add 5% WOF in scour/soap and 2% soda ash to the washing machine.

3. Add your fabric and begin the hottest setting of your washing machine.

4. Once the cycle is complete, you can move on to the mordanting process (see pages 41–52).

SCOURING PLANT/CELLULOSE FABRIC USING A POT

You will need
- Dry fabric
- Kitchen scale
- Soda ash
- Cellulose scour or synthrapol
- Large stainless-steel pot

1. Weigh the dry fabric.

2. Measure 2% soda ash and add it to a jar with a ¼ cup (60 ml) of cold water to wet it out, then add 1 cup (235 ml) boiling water to dissolve it.

3. Fill a pot ¾ of the way with cool water. This amount will be based on the amount of fiber that you are working with. Make sure there is enough room for the fiber to move freely in the water and not cause it to overflow once the fabric is added. I generally use a large 14-quart pot for most projects but of course a smaller pot is ok for smaller endeavors. Add your dissolved soda ash to the pot and place it on the heat.

4. Measure 5% WOF in scour/synthrapol and add it to the pot.

5   Add your fabric and let it sit on a high simmer for 1 hour. Do not allow to boil. Remove the fabric from the heat and leave to cool.

6   Rinse, and you are ready to mordant the fabric (see pages 41–52).

SCOURING SILK FABRIC

You will need
- Dry fabric
- Kitchen scale
- Soda ash
- pH-neutral or gentle detergent
- Large pot

1   Weigh your dry fabric.

2   Measure 1–2% soda ash and add it to a jar with ¼ cup (60 ml) cold water to wet it out, then add 1 cup (235 ml) boiling water to dissolve it.

3   Measure 2% WOF in pH-neutral or gentle detergent.

4   Fill a large pot approximately ¾ with water and place it on the heat. Be sure to leave enough room so that your fabric can move freely without overflowing.

5   Add both the wetted-out soda ash and detergent to the pot. Next, add your fabric and let it sit on the heat at a high simmer for 30 minutes to 1 hour. Do not allow it to boil.

6   Remove the fabric, rinse in cool water, and proceed to mordanting. If the water is very dingy or gray, you may need to repeat the process.

MORDANTING FABRIC

Mordanting is how we bond pigment to fiber. Without mordanting, colors will look dull, turn brown, and fade soon after washing. It is important to note that mordanting does not guarantee that the flower or leaf will bond to the fiber and last indefinitely. Each botanical has its own natural dye constituents that will determine how effective the mordanting process will be.

Experimentation is key in determining whether or not the plant has good inherent natural dye properties. The best way to determine this is to do your own research and discover what is working best. If you want to test the fastness of your plant pigment, mordant and dye your fabric then wash it repeatedly. You can also hang your piece in a sunny location to test its lightfast qualities. Keep a control that is free from light and washing, which you can use as a comparison. You can also perform a rub test, where you create friction on the print to determine if it can withstand wear and tear.

Here we will look at mordanting plant fibers and animal fibers (with and without tannin), mordanting with milk, and mordanting paper (internal and external mordant).

MORDANTING WITH TANNIN: PLANT FIBERS

To get the maximum bond between pigment and plant fiber, you will need to soak your fabric in tannin before moving on to the mordant. Tannin will give you deep, rich colors, which will ultimately give you the greatest results when hammering on plant fibers.

Tannin is abundantly found in many different plants throughout nature. Tannins come in many types and colors, ranging from pinks to yellows and browns and even clear. However, even "clear" tannins will leave color on your projects so it is important to know what color your tannin will create before you begin. Do a test swatch to get clear results.

Tannin can be sourced in a number of places, through foraging, purchasing, or saving. Oak galls, staghorn sumac leaves, and birch are examples of good sources of tannin that can be foraged in nature. You can collect these items and create a simple tannin bath by covering them with water and simmering. Alternatively, you can buy tannins in both ground and extract form from online suppliers. You could also consider saving pomegranate rinds or tea bags – these items can be accumulated over time and are a great source of tannin.

After scouring your plant fiber (see pages 39-40), for example cotton, linen, hemp, and bamboo, follow the below steps to soak it in a tannin bath and mordant it.

Pro Tip
Tannin WOF can vary. If you purchase your tannin commercially, the retailer will tell you the proper WOF to use. If making your own, I have found 10-15% to be a good starting point for most tannins.

You will need
- Dry plant-fiber fabric
- Kitchen scale
- Tannin
- Large stainless-steel pot large enough for your fabric to move freely. Once you are finished with the tannin bath you can empty it for use with the mordant.
- Spoons for stirring
- Potassium alum sulfate
- Soda ash
- Containers for mixing

GETTING STARTED

1 Make a tannin bath using 15% WOF of your material.

2 Add your fabric to the tannin bath and let the temperature rise to a medium-high heat for 1 hour. Too much heat will cause damage to the tannin, so do not let it boil.

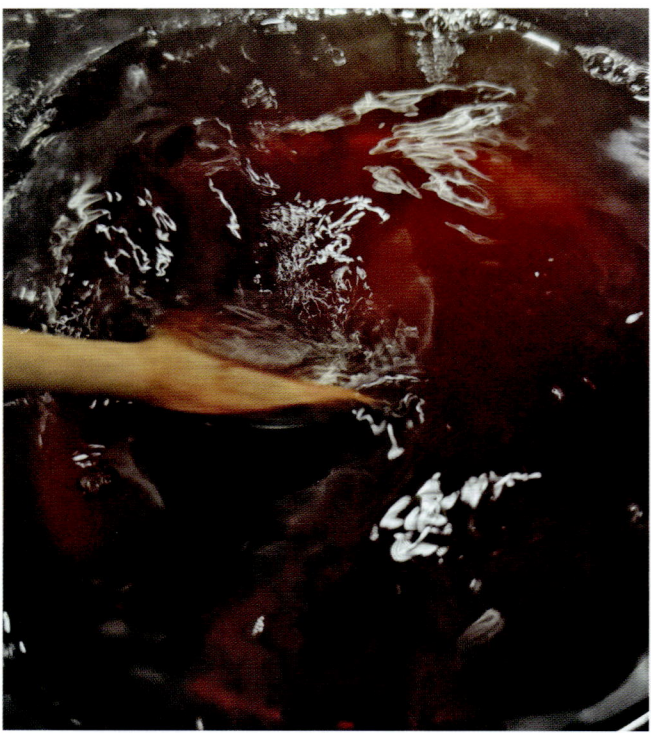

3 Stir the material occasionally to keep the fabric moving so there is even uptake of color and tannin.

4 Turn off the heat and let the material cool to room temperature.

5 Once cool, rinse the fabric in cool water to remove any tannin that has not bonded to the fiber. You can now proceed to the next step: mordanting with alum and soda ash. You do not need to dry the material in between.

6 Calculate 20% WOF for alum (use this high percentage to achieve the best color results) and 10% WOF for soda ash (this will enhance your colors).

7 Fill your pot with water and place on a medium heat on the burner.

8 In a separate container, pour in the alum and mix with approximately 2 cups (470 ml) warm water until dissolved. Pour into your large pot.

9 Add your soda ash to the container and mix with water until dissolved, then pour into your large pot. The soda ash will bubble up, especially if the water is too hot, so do be sure the water is still only warm.

10 Bring the heat up to just under a boil. Let the fabric stay at this temperature, stirring occasionally, for 1.5–2 hours.

11 Remove the pot from the heat, and allow the fabric to cool in the bath, preferably overnight. It is important to let the fabric completely cool so that it allows the alum to properly fix to the fiber.

12 Remove the fabric from the mixture and rinse in a bucket with cool water.

13 Remove the fabric from the bucket. You can now either choose to create a dye bath and give the piece an all-over color (see page 64) or dry the fabric and proceed to flower hammering (see page 36).

Pro Tip
You can mordant your fabric well in advance and store it away in a container until you are ready to use it. I like to mordant my fabric over the winter months so it is ready in the spring/summer and I only have to wait to create until the flowers start blooming.

MORDANTING WITHOUT TANNIN: PLANT AND ANIMAL FIBERS

If you want to keep the background of the piece you are working on as true to the original color as possible, mordant with alum acetate as you will not need a tannin. This is also the best option when mordanting silk.

The drawback of working with alum acetate is that it is an incredibly fine powder, which makes it difficult to work with and measure. When you disturb alum acetate from its container, it will float and disperse into the air. It is imperative that you wear a proper dust mask when working with alum acetate so as not to breathe in these small particles. It is also important to note that you should not mix alum acetate around animals and children.

Alum acetate will produce beautiful, bright results, but mordanting without tannin is a slightly more advanced process due to the care you must take when working with a fine powder.

You will need
- Dry plant- or animal-fiber fabric
- Kitchen scales
- Dust mask
- Rubber gloves
- Alum acetate
- Containers for mixing
- Whisk
- Pot large enough for your fabric to move freely
- Ferrous sulfate
- Spoons for stirring
- Calcium carbonate

1 Weigh your fiber and calculate the alum acetate at 10% WOF. For example, if your fabric weighs 6¼ oz (175 g), you will need ⅝ oz (17.5 g) of alum acetate.

2 Slowly add the alum acetate to a container with 1 cup (235 ml) very hot, but not boiling water and whisk to combine.

3   Take the dissolved alum acetate mixture and add to a large dye pot filled ¾ of the way with hot water. Add a pinch of ferrous sulfate to your mordant and add your fabric.

Pro Tip
If you are not using a tannin, the addition of ferrous sulfate (iron) will increase the permanence and durability of your prints and deepen the shades (see page 55). Do not add more than a small pinch as too much will shift your final prints to a much darker hue, unless that is desired.

4   The water should be the temperature of very hot tap water; you do not want it too hot, as this can be damaging to the mordant. Let the fabric stay in the pot for a few hours, stirring occasionally, then remove and rinse.

5   You will then need to prepare a calcium carbonate or "chalk" bath. This "afterbath" will help to activate the alum and produce a better bond. Measure out 5% WOF.

6   Add the calcium carbonate to a jar with very hot water and whisk to dissolve. Then add it to a bucket of cold water, large enough to hold your fabric. Soak the fabric in the solution and allow it to sit for 20–30 minutes.

7   Rinse the fabric and move on to an all-over dye (see page 64) or dry the fabric to use for hammering (see page 36).

MORDANTING WITH MILK

If you are working with children, don't want to use a metal salt, or are just looking for a simple mordant recipe, consider using milk to mordant your fabric. Although "technically" not a mordant because a chemical reaction does not occur, milk is a good choice for many projects — a great option for binding pigment to fiber that can yield some fantastic results. The process is quite simple but does take some time. So, if you are anxious to start working, this method is a little slower than the other mordanting options mentioned.

Consider the size of your project, what is readily available to you, and what makes the most sense economically and environmentally when choosing a milk to work with. You can purchase milk, such as cow's, sheep, or soy milk, or even make your own soy milk. If you purchase or source other milk products, make sure they are unsweetened with minimal additional ingredients, such as sugar. All dairy milks that are high in protein will work well, regardless of fat content, but do not use nut, oat, or coconut milk. I generally choose soy milk, unless I have a small project and a small amount of dairy milk available that is nearing its expiry date but has not spoiled that I want to use up.

Once cured, you can hammer your flowers onto the fiber. You will find that the fabric will retain the colors and shapes very nicely. This will still be less effective than using alum or ferrous sulfate, but it is far better than not treating the fiber at all. I find that this process gives me the truest colors, in terms of the original color of the flowers, when hammering. This is also the best process to use when working with Japanese indigo (Persicaria tinctoria).

You will need
- Dry fabric
- Milk
- Large bucket, depending on how much fabric you are mordanting
- Fabric
- Spoon for stirring

1. Scour your fabric (see pages 38–40).

2. Make a 1:2 solution of water to milk. So, for every 1 cup (235 ml) or vessel of milk (A), you will need 2 cups (470 ml) or vessels of water (B). I often reuse jars for my measuring containers. It is best if your fabric is still wet from the scouring process; if it is not, pre-wet your fabric to ensure even uptake and coating of the fibers.

3. Cover your mixture and soak the fabric in it overnight.

4. Remove the fabric and squeeze out the excess liquid, but do not rinse it. You can spin out the excess moisture in your washing machine if you like.

5. Lay the fabric flat to dry. If you hang it, you run the risk of a greater concentration of the binder at the bottom of the project, which can result in uneven results, especially when using a dye bath for all-over color prior to hammering your flowers.

6 Once your fabric has completely dried, place the fabric back into the milk mixture, adding more water and milk if necessary to cover it. Soak for 1 hour, then remove and dry.

7 Repeat Step 6 twice more, as long as the milk has not spoiled. The more times you coat the fiber, the better color retention and overall fastness you will have. Once you are done with this process, properly dispose of the milk. Don't leave the mixture in the heat or sunlight; it cannot be reused.

8 Spin the fabric in your washing machine to remove all excess moisture. Allow to fully dry. Leave the fabric in an airtight container and place it out of sunlight for 1-2 weeks to cure.

MORDANTING PAPER

Paper is more durable than you might expect. As long as you work carefully, you can wet many types of paper without damage. You will not need to scour paper. You do, however, need to mordant it in order for the colors to be bright, bold, and long lasting.

Just like fabric, not all paper is created equal. Many fine art papers contain sizing, which can be helpful in traditional printing techniques. It can slow down absorption of water or pigment and create sharper, cleaner prints. The sizing can be a range of substances depending on the intended final use of the paper. It is important to keep this in mind if you are not achieving your desired results, as the paper itself may contain something that prevents the pigment from getting into the fiber, so you may need to change your mordanting method and/or your paper.

Paper can be mordanted in one of two ways:

1. With an external or spot mordant, where mordant is brushed onto the surface and left to dry.
2. With an internal mordant, where the paper is submerged into the mordant.

Both techniques will give great results and can be interchanged as necessary.

OPTION 1: EXTERNAL MORDANT

This method requires you to simply sponge brush the dissolved mordant onto the paper. I use this technique when I am working with delicate paper or surfaces that I don't think could handle being submerged. I sometimes only need a small portion of paper to have the mordant on, so it doesn't need full submersion — in that case, I will "spot" mordant.

You can weigh your paper as you would fabric to get the proper measurements. However, if you are working on a small project, this may be tricky. I often double the recipe below if working on a large amount of heavy paper, such as greeting cards. I like a very strong mixture when working this way to ensure I am getting enough of the solution into the fiber of the paper to increase the intensity of the prints.

You will need
- Potassium alum sulfate
- Kitchen scale
- Large jar, enough to hold 2 cups (470 ml) of water, with a wide-enough mouth to fit your sponge brush
- Soda ash
- Small jar
- Sponge brush
- Paper
- Absorbent cloth

1. Add ½ oz (15 g) potassium alum sulfate to ¼ cup (60 ml) very hot or boiling tap water in your two-cup jar to dissolve.

2. Add ⅛ oz (5 g) of soda ash to ¼ cup (60 ml) warm tap water in your small jar, and stir to dissolve.

3. Add the dissolved soda ash to the jar with the alum in it. If the alum water is still very hot, the soda ash will bubble up and over; let it cool before adding it. Fill the 2-cup (475-ml) jar the rest of the way with hot – not boiling – water.

4. Dip your sponge brush into the solution and apply a thin coat to the surface or selected area of the paper that you want to mordant, moving in one direction until the entire sheet is covered (A). Particularly for more fragile papers, be sure not to flood the surface. Lay a paper towel over the top and gently pat dry (if you want to mordant further sheets in a batch, you can layer them up on top of this).

Pro Tip
The mixture should be used and then disposed of. If it is kept, you run the risk of the alum bonding to the soda ash, and it will no longer work the way it was intended.

5 Allow it to dry completely on the absorbent cloth, then add a second coat (B).

OPTION 2: INTERNAL MORDANT

As long as you work carefully, you can fully submerge many types of paper. These papers can also be used for eco printing, where you steam the botanicals into the paper to create beautiful colors and prints. This is a much quicker and easier process than mordanting fabric.

This method will require all of the same materials as Option 1. The only difference is that you will make a larger batch and will submerge the paper into the mordant. This will give really beautiful, saturated colors when you print. When I mordant paper, I generally try to process a variety of papers – I mordant bookmarks, gift tags, and greeting cards all in the same batch. Do not saturate thin, delicate papers like rice paper.

When it comes to soaking the paper, 15-20 minutes is a guideline, but it is ok to leave it for longer — the paper will survive! I have left paper overnight and it has not dissolved. Experiment with longer soak times as this will change your final results. Heavier-weight paper, such as watercolor and mixed media, can take longer exposure to water and will not break down. In fact, in cases where sizing has been added to the paper, a longer soaking will help remove it so that more of the solution will penetrate the paper, offering bolder, brighter end results. Give it a try and compare your results!

You will need

- Paper for mordanting
- Alum
- Soda ash
- Kitchen scale
- Tray or roasting pan, large enough to fit your papers and mordant
- Towels, paper towels, or scrap fabric

1. To mordant around 1¾ oz (50 g) of paper, use 1 oz (30 g) of alum, ⅜ oz (10 g) of soda ash and 3 cups (700 ml) of hot water (or enough to fill the pan without overflowing once the paper is added). Mix each of the above in a jar with hot water to dissolve, then pour into the tray that will hold your papers.

Pro Tip
You want enough hot water in the tray to submerge and soak your paper. Add more water if needed to ensure the papers are soaking below the surface of the tray.

2. Lay each sheet of paper in the tray, one at a time, making sure that they get saturated.

3 Leave the paper in the tray for approximately 15–20 minutes, or longer if desired.

4 Gently remove each sheet of paper and lay it out on an absorbent surface, such as a towel or paper towels. Do not let the sheets overlap or touch each other. You can then lay a towel over the top and gently press to remove any additional moisture. You can also stack the papers with paper towels or scrap fabric in between the layers and place a weight on top to help them dry as flat as possible.

5 Once the paper is completely dry, it is ready to hammer (see page 36).

Ironing paper

If you are anxious to use your paper right away and cannot wait for it to dry, follow these steps to iron it – most paper is a natural fiber after all! I have also found that paper such as cardstock, which I use for cards, bookmarks, and gift tags, generally needs to be ironed after the mordanting process.

You will need
- Mordanted paper
- Absorbent cloth
- Large sponge or towel
- Iron
- Cover cloth
- Lidded container

1 Remove the soaked paper from the tray and place it onto an absorbent cloth. Blot any additional moisture up with a large sponge or towel.

2 Place a cloth over the paper and iron it on a cotton setting. You will notice a lot of steam as you iron — this is the moisture evaporating from the paper. Be careful not to apply too much heat so that you do not scorch the paper.

Pro Tip

If your paper is already dry but has wrinkles, you can use a spray bottle to mist it with water and continue with the ironing process as above.

3. Keep going, until the paper is dry and flat, occasionally checking on the paper to see if it is dry by pulling back the cover cloth.

4. Store the paper away in a container with a lid for safekeeping. Keep in mind that the paper is highly susceptible to staining once it has been treated.

USING MODIFIERS

Modifiers change the original color of the petals to give a broad spectrum of hues from one flower. By changing the pH of a natural dye, especially dyes that are fugitive (don't adhere well) or contain anthocyanin (purple, red, and blue pigment), you can shift them to completely different colors quite simply. You can use natural household ingredients, such as lemon juice, to make the color more acidic or basic, causing a shift in hue.

Pro Tip
Squeeze a small amount of lemon or lime juice into a dish and use it to paint directly onto the textile or paper with a paintbrush. You can also dilute the citric acid with a small amount of water to make it more fluid when painting.

ABOVE These heart shapes were punched from rose petals and hammered onto the fabric.

TOP RIGHT AND BOTTOM RIGHT Rose petal hearts are modified with lemon juice, turning the pigment from purple to pink. The result is a magical transformation of color.

I hammered eight Rose Coral coreopsis flowers onto paper and painted over the top of them with a range of modifiers mixed with water to illustrate how different modifiers can change the colors of certain natural pigments. Each one changed the original color of the flower to give a broad spectrum of hues from a single flower. In this case, the higher the acidity, the pinker the hue, therefore highly acidic lemon juice formed the pinkest hue. The higher the alkalinity, the more yellow the hue, therefore alkaline soda ash formed the most yellow hue. Those falling more toward the middle of the pH scale had a less dramatic, more subdued shift.

Lemon juice, baking soda, alum, soda ash, iron (ferrous sulfate), copper, and titanium oxalate were all used as modifiers on eight hammered Rose Coral coreopsis flowers, with one hammered without a modifier for comparison.

FERROUS SULFATE (IRON WATER)

Ferrous sulfate is a great natural resource that will increase the fastness of your natural dye project. It can also be used as a natural mordant or modifier in the dye process. This means you can use ferrous sulfate both as a stand-alone mordant, or you can use it on finished work to adjust the final color of your project.

Iron will have a strong reaction to the tannins found in plants and will darken or "sadden" the hue. This can be both a desirable and an undesirable effect, based on the results you are looking to achieve. Iron can also be destructive to delicate fabrics when used in too large a quantity or when it is not washed out of the fabric quickly enough.

Iron water can be made in a few ways. You can purchase ferrous sulfate, which comes in a crystalized form. A small amount goes a long way, and this is a purer way to work with iron water, eliminating the need for creating a rusty solution with bits of old metal. Ferrous sulfate and/or rust water should be used with caution; always wear gloves, use a dust mask, and keep it out of reach of children and pets.

Alternatively, it is easy to make your own iron water. Simply find a large jar and fill it with rusty items or items you can rust. Old nails, gears, tools, and cans all work well. Some items will not rust due to an anti-rust surface. I prefer to find and use items that are already rusty — that way I am sure they will work well.

Collect rusty items to make iron water to use for future natural dye and modification of projects.

Fill your jar with equal parts white vinegar and water and allow it to sit and soak on a shelf. Once the water starts to look murky and orange, you can use it to create with. You can also continue to refill the jar with more water and vinegar so that the metal items continue to rust.

USING FERROUS SULFATE ON SUMAC LEAVES

Often considered a weed, Staghorn sumac is a tremendous natural dye plant, which is high in tannin. It is great for creating shapes with a paper punch to hammer (see page 148), as well as for beautiful hammered leaves. When soaked in a bath of ferrous sulfate, the leaf print turns from green to a beautiful gray shade, and the fabric has increased fastness, along with additional tolerance to direct sunlight, washing, and daily wear and tear.

Ferrous sulfate in its powdered form is a light greenish-blue color, consisting of crystals similar to salt. Once added to hot water, the solution will eventually turn a rusty brown color and will be ready to use as soon as it has dissolved.

To use ferrous sulfate on sumac leaves, place the hammered leaf fabric in a bath of teaspoon (6 g) of ferrous sulfate to 3 cups (700 ml) of hot water to shift the color from green to gray. After a quick soak in the ferrous sulfate bath, remove the fabric and wash it in cold water with dish soap. Dry and iron the final piece.

ABOVE *Staghorn sumac leaves.*

TOP RIGHT *The sumac leaf is pulled back to reveal a perfect print after being hammered.*

BOTTOM RIGHT *The sumac printed fabric soaking in a ferrous sulfate bath.*

FAR RIGHT *I like how this slub linen fabric adds texture to these prints. I think this print and fabric combination would make a fantastic pair of curtains.*

WASHING AND AFTERCARE

After your piece has been fully designed and hammered, wait for it to dry completely, then iron it. Use the appropriate heat setting for your fiber, and iron the back of the prints, then turn the fabric over and iron the front.

To eliminate color run-off on the white areas of your project and keep everything as clean as possible, after a few days (or even weeks), rinse the fabric in a bucket of clean cool water with pH-neutral or gentle soap and then immediately rinse again in a second bucket of clean cool water. Waiting to wash the fabric will allow for a better bond between the pigment and fiber. However, if you used iron in your mordant, you can wash your fiber once the prints are completely dry, after you have ironed them.

Naturally dyed fabrics should be treated gently, as you would with any delicate fabric. This work is now a piece of art and should be treated as such! It should be washed as little as possible, by hand, with cold water and a pH-neutral soap. The piece should be left to dry flat and be kept out of direct sunlight to minimize fading.

Although the fabrics have undergone mordanting, their prints will still have a gradual fade over time, depending on their unique fastness. The good news is that the mordanted fabric is now treated for the life of the fabric, so you can continue to add flowers and prints to a piece year after year.

If you do not mordant your fabric, some prints will turn brown and wash out very quickly. Keep this in mind when you begin a new project on fabric, especially if you put a lot of hours of hammering into the piece.

Paper projects or wall art should also be stored or hung out of direct sunlight, where possible. If you frame the art, use UV-protected glass.

Freshly hammered flower prints are left to dry on the clothes line just before a summer sunset. Warm summer nights are perfect for drying freshly hammered fabric.

PART TWO
THE PROJECTS

PROJECTS ON FABRIC

Projects on fabric can be a fun and rewarding way to elevate your clothing, accessories, or home decor. Hammering flowers and leaves is a simple way to take a piece of fabric that may be dull, stained, or blank, and transform it into something special that will be valued and appreciated for years to come.

For example, the table runners found in this section were not anything special, but – after the addition of hammered leaves and flowers – became unique pieces that bring me joy to use, and are lovely to look at all year long.

Alternatively, I enjoy taking fabric that was once ordinary or stained, and giving it a new look and story. A hammered flower stripe or perfectly placed leaf print can create a sense of whimsy that will bring a smile to your face each time you see it. Dive into the world of fabrics and uncover the limitless possibilities they hold – it's a journey that never gets old!

Hammered flowers on cotton canvas.

TREASURE POUCHES

Pouches are great for gift wrapping, party favors, or for holding keepsakes and found objects. I have always enjoyed collecting tiny curiosities when I am hiking, at the beach, or just enjoying the outdoors. I look for the most interesting pebble, a pretty fragment of washed-up sea glass, or some other little piece of color inspiration that captures my attention. These pouches are perfect for keeping these treasures tucked away in a safe place.

Blank pouches are available through various online retailers (see page 158) and come in a variety of sizes. The small blank surfaces allow for endless creativity. The most important detail is that they are 100% natural fiber and not synthetic. To achieve the best results, they must first be scoured (see pages 38-40) and mordanted (see pages 41-52), then you can begin to design and print them however you choose, for any occasion. You can create shapes and patterns with the flower petals and leaves, or simply hammer one or more flowers. If you want to change the color of your pouch, I recommend dyeing it before you hammer the flowers. A variety of flowers and leaves were used to create the pouches pictured, including cosmos, coreopsis, bidens, pansies, hemp, and Japanese indigo leaves.

A variety of hammered flower pouches dyed with Japanese indigo.

Optional: dyeing the fabric pouches

The pouches pictured were first tied with rubber bands and dyed in a Japanese indigo 1,2,3 vat to attain the blue color. This is one of the easiest ways to create a traditional indigo vat for dyeing fabric. The vat uses indigo pigment, calcium hydroxide for elevating pH, and fructose for reducing oxygen. This process is a little more involved than making a dye bath with flowers. It is, however, a worthwhile experience if you choose to explore the wonder of natural blue dye, one of the oldest and most magical dyes on record. Traditional indigo dyeing is an art all by itself. I encourage you to learn and discover more about this process.

Hammered flowers on indigo-dyed pouches.

Alternatively, you could naturally dye the pouches any color you wish by making a dye bath by simmering and extracting color from flowers or leaves of your choice. The longer the soak time and the more plants you use, the more saturated the color will be.

Total hammering time
30 minutes+, depending on the quantity of pouches

You will need
- Parchment or similar paper
- Cotton canvas pouches
- Wooden flat surface or cutting board
- Variety of flowers
- Cover cloth
- Rubber mallet

1 Place a piece of parchment paper inside the pouch to stop the pigment from bleeding onto the back of the project. Make sure the pouch lies flat on your hammering surface so that the flower will hammer evenly without a crease.

2 Arrange the flowers (and leaves, if using) onto the surface of the pouch. Lay them face down to ensure you get the best possible print.

3 Place a cover cloth over the flowers (and leaves) and hammer precisely with the rubber mallet, tapping each one in a clockwise motion.

4 Once all flowers (and leaves) are flat and secure against the surface and there are no visible unhammered petals, gently remove them from the pouch to reveal your finished product.

LEFT *Petals and leaves were placed on the fabric one at a time to create this mandala pouch. The surrounding yellow/orange dye color was created by rubbing marigold petals directly onto the fabric to release their pigment.*

ABOVE *Pouches in use, holding memories of summer.*

GARMENT PATCHES

I adore making patches. They are a great way to explore a variety of botanicals and get your creativity flowing without the sometimes-overwhelming nature of larger-scale projects. Patches can be created in a variety of sizes simply by tearing fabric to create rustic frayed-edge squares or rectangles. Most fabrics will tear easily, without a lot of force; cotton canvas requires a little more effort but will still tear.

You may choose to print either a solitary flower or leaf on a patch, or alternatively arrange multiple botanical elements together. The patches can also be enhanced with embroidery, stencils, or acrylic paint, based on individual preference. Decorated patches are ideal for enhancing jeans, jackets, or backpacks. Alternatively, they can be treated as miniature works of art, suitable for framing or affixing to greeting cards. I like to make a set of patches to put aside and use for various applications at later dates.

Patches are delightful small-scale projects with endless possibilities.

Total hammering time
Less than 1 hour

You will need
- Medium-weight cotton canvas
- Fabric scissors
- Variety of flowers
- Cover cloth
- Wooden flat surface or cutting board
- Regular hammer
- Fabric Mod Podge® sealer
- Iron (optional)
- Stencils (optional)
- Sponge brush

1. Mordant your fabric following the instructions for Mordanting with tannin: plant fibers (see pages 41–43) and allow it to dry.

2. To tear the fabric, first cut a small slit in your cotton canvas, about 2–3 in (5–7.5 cm) from the edge, depending on the size of patch you would like to work with. Next, grab the fabric at each side of the slit and pull until you have a long strip. The act of tearing will create a frayed, rustic edge. You can remove any stray threads by pulling them away from the weave of the fabric and discarding them.

3. Take the long strip and turn it horizontally. You can now decide how big to make your patch. Here, I went about 2 in (5 cm) from the edge of my strip and cut another small slit. Just like before, I grabbed the fabric at each side of the slit and pulled to get a square patch.

4. Continue this process until you have a pile of patches ready for designing. You can now decide how you would like to design them. For this patch, I used a few flowers from my garden that were varieties of coreopsis and cosmos.

5 Arrange the flowers face down on the garment patch and place your cover cloth over the top. Use your rubber mallet to hammer them one at a time, then remove the hammered flowers and allow them to dry.

6 You can use an iron to heat-set the patches. Next, use your sponge brush to apply the fabric sealer (Mod Podge®) over the top of the design. It will appear cloudy at first but will dry clear. The curing time for this sealer is 1–2 weeks, so be sure not to wash the patches before then.

7 Now sew the patches onto your garments – especially items such as backpacks and denim jackets, or any place you don't plan on washing immediately. After my patches were fully dry, I sewed them onto my favorite pair of overalls using a simple whipstitch to tie the two fabrics together. You do not need to wait for the patches to cure before applying them; however, you cannot wash the item until you have waited 1–2 weeks.

Optional: Designing with stencils

You can use flowers to add stenciled designs to your project. Here, I cut the shape of a vase out of stencil plastic (see page 138) and placed the stencil plastic over the top of the fabric patch. I then rubbed a Black Knight scabiosa flower across the top of the stencil to transfer the pigment onto the fabric. I used the printed vase shape to build up my design, hammering flowers above the mouth of the vase and adding a few hammered leaves and stems.

You can purchase precut stencils online or at craft stores (see page 158). You can often find simple shapes such as squares, circles, or patterns, which work great for this process and add a textured design element to your project. You can also finish the project with embroidery (see page 147), acrylic paint, or homemade natural pigment inks.

A stencil was used above to create the harlequin design and vase shape, by rubbing Japanese indigo leaves and Black Knight scabiosa petals onto the fabric, prior to hammering the flowers on.

HAND-TORN RIBBONS

Ribbons are super fun to make and can be used for all kinds of applications, including gift wrapping, hair accessories, and home decor. You can wrap them around wreaths or create a ribbon banner. I like to have them on hand for when I need a special addition to something I'm gifting.

Making ribbons is a great way to get children involved. Fun to tear and easy to create, these ribbons can be made out of any natural-fiber fabric – the act of ripping the fabric will give you a lovely frayed, rustic edge too. I used silk velvet for this project, but I also like using linen, silk, and densely woven cotton fabric to make these. In general, I will first scour (see pages 38–40) and mordant the fabric (see pages 41–52) and allow it to dry before printing. Ribbons generally do not experience a lot of washing and light exposure, making them good candidates for exploring fabric that is not mordanted. They also offer a good opportunity to explore botanicals that may not be as colorfast as others you will work with. Experiment and explore!

Total hammering time
1+ hours, depending on the quantity and length of your ribbons

You will need
- Natural-fiber fabric, available by the yard
- Fabric scissors
- Tape measure
- Flowers or leaves
- Cover cloth
- Regular hammer or rubber mallet
- Wooden flat surface or cutting board

1. Decide how wide you would like the ribbon strip to be. A good width for ribbons is usually around 1.5–2 in (4–5 cm). Measure or estimate the size you want and cut a small slit into the fabric. (Sometimes I don't care about the exact width as much, and just create a bunch of strips at random to give me lots of options for final use at a later time.)

2. Continue to cut small slits up the edge of the fabric, marking how wide each ribbon will be and how many you will be creating.

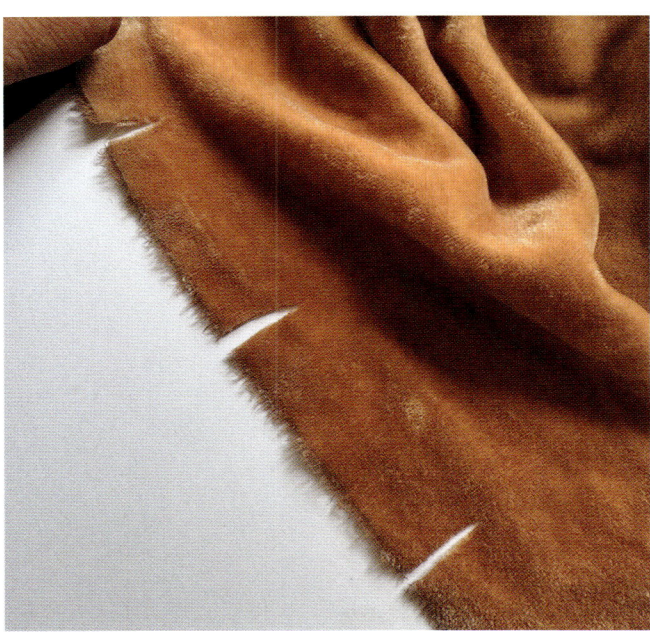

3   Grab the cloth at each side of the slit and pull. The fabric will tear, creating a long strip. Repeat this process until you have all the ribbons you will be hammering onto.

4   Once you have created all the strips, decide which flowers and leaves you will add and hammer the patterns in place (see page 36). I generally hammer full flowers in a row; however, you can also move to the edges of the ribbon to create the feeling of a more developed surface design. I like to use the same flowers in repetition, to give the ribbon a cohesive feel, but you might try alternating two or three different flowers if you don't have many of the same variety. You could also consider adding individual petals into the surrounding negative space.

BOTTOM LEFT *The ribbon with the white background was created on fabric that has not been pretreated. The colors are still vibrant – they will stay that way with little washing and light exposure.*

BELOW *Finished hammered flower ribbons ready to be used.*

RIGHT *A hammered flower ribbon being used to decorate a present.*

PROJECTS ON FABRIC

COSMOS GARDEN SOCKS

Yes, you can even print flowers on socks! They take to flower hammering exceptionally well, coming in a variety of materials, fabrics, and textures. Just be sure to find a nice natural fabric with minimal synthetic fibers added (a small amount of spandex or stretch is ok). Here, I used a bamboo pair. The socks can be designed in so many ways, based on your own preferences and the availability of flowers in your area.

Total hammering time
Less than 1.5 hours

You will need
- Cardstock or paper to fit inside the sock
- Natural-fiber socks
- Cosmos flowers
- Craft scissors
- Regular hammer
- Cover cloth
- Wooden flat surface or cutting board
- Sumac leaves (optional)
- Paper punch (optional)

LEFT *A freshly picked bouquet of Chocolate cosmos, Desert Coral coreopsis and Candystripe cosmos.*

RIGHT *Add a touch of whimsy to your outfit with a pair of hammered flower socks.*

GETTING STARTED

1. Put a piece of heavyweight cardstock or paper inside each sock so the hammered flowers do not bleed through. Push it all the way into the toes and move it up as necessary while working.

2. Trim your flowers to size using craft scissors, if needed, before hammering. I trimmed the middle of my Chocolate cosmos flowers down to remove some of their bulkiness, which would have caused messy prints.

3. Using a regular hammer and cover cloth, hammer your flowers onto the socks (see page 36), starting at the toe area. Make sure that the flower is fully transferred and the petals are flat against the sock after being pounded.

4. Build up the flower prints, alternating between your varieties.

5   Continue to hammer up the socks, adding leaves and flowers as desired until they are completely filled with flowers. You can repeat the process for the bottom of the socks as well.

Optional: Punched shapes

I used a small paper punch and a sumac leaf to create leaf shapes, and I like what the little sprig added to the mix. I hammered them in between the flowers to add a broader range of color and give more interest to the design. You could continue to experiment with this idea by adding in other leaf or bug shapes; even flower-shaped punches would give you another way to build up the elements of your design.

BLACK HOLLYHOCK BUTTERFLY BANDANNA

Hollyhocks are enjoyable to hammer. They come in lots of colors and offer tons of beautiful blooms to work with. My absolute favorite are Blacknight hollyhocks. The petals are a deep burgundy color that appears almost black in the garden. The petals themselves are a little tougher in texture than some of the other flowers I mention in this book. For that reason, I think it would be best to explore the use of both a rubber mallet and a regular hammer to see which will work best for you.

Hollyhocks are biennial flowers, meaning that they will put down roots and grow foliage in the first year and produce flowers in the second. They will not continue to come back, although they will reseed themselves if you let the flowers go to seed. So, if you plant them this season, you won't have flowers until the following year. I recommend planting new flowers consistently over many years so that you can always have these beauties in your garden as they are spectacular. They are an excellent source of natural dye, and the pollinators love them. Hollyhocks are prone to plant disease called "rust," so be on the lookout for an orangey, rust-like substance that appears on the leaves. You will need to cut away the affected leaves and spray them with neem oil.

Total hammering time
Less than 1 hour

You will need
- Mordanting equipment and materials (see page 41)
- Hollyhock or black hollyhock flowers
- Bandanna or fabric
- Cover cloth
- Regular hammer
- Wooden flat surface or cutting board
- Cosmos flowers
- Iron water or ferrous sulfate
- Watercolor size 8 brush
- Paper towel

1. It is important to mordant your fabric with a tannin for this project. Follow the steps for Mordanting with tannin: plant fibers (see pages 41–43).

Black hollyhocks are stunning.

2 Start by removing the petals from the hollyhocks to create the butterfly shape. Each flower has five petals, and you will need four for each butterfly.

3 Place the petals symmetrically on the project fabric – two on each side – to determine their placement. You can leave a small space between the wings where the body of the butterfly will go.

4 When you are ready to hammer the petals, place them face down on the wooden hammering surface. Next, lay the cover cloth over the first petal and hammer the entire surface (see page 36). Repeat this process three more times to create the full butterfly shape.

Pro Tip
Hollyhock petals tend to be a little tough, so you may need to peek behind the cover cloth to ensure you have hammered the entire shape.

5 Add a few additional cosmos flowers in the same way, to make it feel like the butterflies are fluttering around a garden.

6. Because this fabric was mordanted for cotton and has been treated with tannin in Step 1, you can now use iron water or ferrous sulfate to naturally paint lines that will look like the body of the butterfly (see page 81). Once you have made your solution, you can paint on the fabric with your watercolor brush to create the body and antennae. Place a paper towel under the bandanna to soak up any excess moisture. As long as you do not oversaturate the brush, you can paint a nice freeform line that will not spread. Start with a small, thin line and build up to a thicker line by keeping the tip of the brush elevated and gently creating a stroke on the fabric. If you oversaturate the fabric from the start, you will not be able to remove the color.

7. Allow the iron water to fully dry. Normally you should wash ferrous sulfate immediately out of fabric as it can be damaging to the fiber, however, due to the very small amount used here, you may prefer to wait 2 weeks to allow the other prints to cure.

8. Iron the bandanna on a cotton setting to set the color and create more of a bond. It is now ready to be worn.

SUMMER STRIPED LINEN BLOUSE

I love going to thrift shops and yard sales, looking for clothing that I think would be perfect for this process. Items with small stains that can be easily covered by a hammered flower or leaf are great options and are usually heavily discounted for their minor imperfections. Always try to read the fiber content tag to be sure you are getting a natural fiber.

For this piece, I decided to give the blouse an all-over natural dye before I began. Because your project is already mordanted it is ready to accept natural dye in any form, including all-over dyes and bundle dyeing – when you steam your fabric bundled with many varieties of flowers and leaves to create many different colors all over the fabric. I used marigolds to overdye this piece, knowing that the gold produced by the flowers would create yellow-and-green stripes where it overdyed the already present white-and-blue stripes.

For this design, I wanted to keep with the striped theme of the blouse, so I added a row of hammered flowers. I kept it simple by using only one variety of flower and leaf for the stripe, a Sulfur cosmos, which was growing abundantly in my home garden at the time. This basic pattern is a great way to add interest and character to a garment, without having to use a ton of flowers. You could also consider adding small details, such as a single flower, to a collar or sleeve for a flowery pop in just the right place!

Total hammering time
Less than 1–2 hours

You will need
- Marigold flowers and leaves
- Large pot
- Slotted spoon, strainer, or cheesecloth
- Striped linen blouse
- Sulfur cosmos
- Rubber mallet
- Wooden flat surface or cutting board
- Cover cloth

1 Pick a few handfuls of marigold flowers and simmer them in a pot with twice as much water, so that they are covered and there is enough room for the blouse to go in once the flowers have been removed.

2 Let the flowers simmer for about 40 minutes, but do not let them boil – they should stay on the heat until they start to turn from bright orange to beige. Once they look like they have released all of their color into the water, strain them out with a slotted spoon. You could also use a strainer or cheesecloth.

3   Add the striped linen blouse to the water, stirring occasionally. Keep it in the dye bath for 1 hour on a medium-high heat, then turn off the heat and let the bath cool with the blouse in it. (You could leave it overnight for maximum dye retention.)

4   Once cool, rinse the blouse in cold water and let it air dry out of the sun.

5   Using the hammering technique (see page 36), cover each flower with a cover cloth and hammer it onto the fabric using a lightweight rubber mallet.

6   Hammer leaves from the same plant around each flower, going under the stripe.

RIGHT *The end result was a beautiful way to highlight the flower without distracting from the stripes on the blouse.*

VELVET FLOWER SCARF

Who said flowers are only for spring and summer? I adore making items from my summer garden and wearing them through the colder days ahead. My region experiences harsh winters, and having a beautiful flower-filled scarf to wear when the temperature drops is very welcome.

Total hammering time
2-3 hours

You will need
- Mordanting equipment and materials (see page 41)
- Blank silk velvet scarf
- Variety of flowers
- Cover cloth
- Regular hammer
- Wooden flat surface or cutting board

1 Follow the steps for Mordanting with tannin: plant fibers (see pages 41–43), using a powdered sumac tannin bath to achieve the pink color at 15% WOF. Allow to dry.

I wanted the bottom of this beautiful scarf to feel heavy with flowers.

I wanted this scarf to have a background color, so I used sumac tannin to create a dye bath. The outcome is a warm dusty pink hue. You could also consider a yellow tannin, such as pomegranate, or for a more vintage look use a black tea or oak galls as your tannin. Alternatively, mordant without the use of a tannin to keep the background free of additional color.

The use of tannin and mordant gives this scarf a bold, bright, and clear print design. I used a mix of cosmos and coreopsis and I love how each flower can leave a surprising print, for example the Velouette cosmos leaves a beautiful blue outline.

2   Starting with the end of the scarf, hammer the flowers face down, using the technique on page 65. Keep adding flowers to make it feel as though they are piling up at the bottom of each side.

3   After hammering, notice how the flower petals are all semi-translucent and flat against the surface of the fabric. The flower is now ready to peel off the material.

4   Continue to build up the flowers in the same way on each end of the scarf.

5   Add random flowers to the remaining portion of the material so they appear to be floating toward the bottom. The scarf is now ready to wear and enjoy. Allow a minimum of 2 weeks before washing your work.

JAPANESE INDIGO TABLE RUNNER

Japanese indigo (Persicaria tinctoria) is the most magical and intriguing of all of the plants I work with. The leaves are unlike anything else, other than other indigo-bearing plants. Traditionally, you may know indigo for the beautiful midnight blue-purple color we commonly associate with this plant. While it is capable of that, it also can be used in its fresh state to hammer leaves and create incredible turquoise-blue leaf prints. The hammered leaves start off as green and oxidize to turquoise. Once rinsed and washed, a bright turquoise blue emerges.

Indigo can be grown quite easily as long as you can provide it with plenty of water, nitrogen-rich soil with regular feedings, and lots of sunlight. I usually grow mine in large containers or I designate a good sunny spot in the garden. Harvest the leaves only as you need them as they will wilt fairly quickly once picked, even if placed in water. Once all of the leaves are harvested, new ones will grow back or you can cut the stems, place them in water and roots will form. You can then plant them and have a full second harvest in the same season.

Fresh leaf Japanese indigo projects are a little different from other hammered leaf/flower projects because they do not technically require a mordant. In fact, you will have long-lasting results on natural fibers as long as they have been pre-scoured (see pages 38–40) and are not left in direct sunlight. Japanese indigo has an affinity to natural fibers, unlike most flower dyes. However, the use of soy milk as both a pre- and post-treatment to the fabric can yield longer-lasting results in terms of fastness (see pages 46–47). The milk will coat the fiber with protein, helping to both bind it and protect it from the elements. Like most natural dyes, even Japanese indigo prints will fade over time if left in direct sunshine. This is why an afterbath of soy milk can help improve lightfastness of the prints.

This table runner was a labor of love, as it took many hours over a few months to complete. Completion time will vary depending on the length of the runner and the number of leaves available to you. I used a hemp-/cotton-blend fabric, 72 x 15 in (183 x 38 cm). I initially worked on this project slowly as the leaves were developing and I quickly realized that this would give me inconsistent color throughout the piece. Leaves that bloom earlier in the season will have significantly less pigment content than those that have experienced the heat of summer. This will mean a lighter shade of turquoise instead of the deeper, more vibrant shade I was seeking. Keep this in mind when you are selecting a project for your Japanese indigo. That being said, I decided to wait until my plants were bushy to develop and finish the prints. The end result is an heirloom piece that can be passed down and cherished for many years to come.

FAR LEFT *Freshly picked Japanese indigo. Hints of blue are already showing in the beautiful leaves.*

LEFT *The hammered leaves on this end of the table runner were from new plants, early in the season. The results were lovely, but the larger leaves did not have as much pigment yet. They did oxidize to blue, but it was not as saturated as the leaves hammered later in the season.*

RIGHT *Table runners are a great way to preserve your summer garden in one special place.*

Total hammering time
5 hours+ (this will vary based on the size of your table runner)

You will need
- Natural-fiber table runner
- Japanese indigo leaves
- Cover cloth
- Rubber mallet
- Wooden flat surface or cutting board

1. Pick your leaves! Keep in mind that you only want to pick what you have time to use in that hammering session. The table runner is a little different from other hammering projects. It is more reliant on technique and learning your individual plants because the entire process is simply repetition of hammering the same leaf over and over (using the technique on page 36).

2. Hammer each leaf completely, and gently peel it away. Working on a large scale can be a bit of a puzzle. You have to keep finding the leaf that is the "best fit" for the vacant space. This means alternating not only between smaller and larger leaves but also the direction that they are pointing in. For this piece, lay a leaf down and make sure it is a good fit before hammering it in place. Keep searching for a leaf that fits the space neatly before moving on to the next print.

3. Make sure that you have covered the entire surface of the cloth with leaves. Look for areas that have too much empty space and fill in with tiny, young leaves. The finished table runner should look like this before it is washed. Once it is laundered, the chlorophyll from the leaves rinses away and the turquoise-blue pigment emerges through oxidation.

4. Allow the piece to dry fully, then iron it using the cotton setting. You can then rinse your finished table runner in cool water and allow it to dry out of the sunlight. Freshly washed Japanese indigo prints reveal their true turquoise blue color (right).

Variables with Japanese indigo leaves

Many variables need to be considered to achieve a uniform and consistent look throughout a large piece.

- The side of the leaf used: I found the earth (or bottom) side of the Japanese indigo leaves gave me the most desirable, bluest print.
- The time of day for picking: Leaves picked in the morning with a little dew on them will leave significantly better prints than those picked at high noon or the evening, which have been out in the sunlight all day.
- The freshness of the leaves: Use your picked leaves as quickly as possible. I try to only pick what I will have time to use for that hammering session, so they do not wilt. Shriveled, droopy leaves will be hard to place and lay flat as you work. The moisture content will decrease, and they will leave a more faded, less desirable print.
- The size of the leaves: Smaller, younger leaves are usually rich with pigment and leave a very blue leaf print.

JAPANESE INDIGO VARIATIONS

A silk tie and silk pillow cover after hammering and before fully oxidizing.

A pleasant surprise! Here, Japanese indigo leaves were hammered onto a hemp/cotton-blend fabric that was pretreated with a soy milk binder. As a result, some of the leaf prints turned a lovely pink-purple shade, known as indirubin; a hue that can be coaxed from indigo under certain conditions, such as using silk fabric or ironing your leaf prints soon after hammering them.

TOMATO TEA TOWEL

This tea towel started off as an experimental project to see if I could achieve beautiful prints from San Marzano tomato leaves. As it turned out, I could. It is an aromatic experience to hammer tomato leaves; they have such a specific smell of summer to me, which holds so many memories of childhood gardening. The end result was a beautiful tea towel, which brought me joy all summer.

Sometimes the projects we create can be just for fun, to create memories with a loved one, or for experimentation. I have washed these prints a few times since creating them and they still look nice; I'm excited to see how they continue to hold up with general wear and tear. You will never know what a plant might reveal to you until you try it!

Total hammering time
1.5 hours

You will need
- Mordanting equipment and materials
- Tea towel
- Tomato leaves
- Cover cloth
- Regular hammer
- Wooden flat surface or cutting board
- Paper and pencil
- Stencil plastic
- X-ACTO® knife
- Orange cosmos flower

1. Mordant your fabric following one of the pretreatment steps on pages 41–52.

2. Start by testing which side of the tomato leaves will give the "best" print. I found that the bottom side against the project fabric worked best. Arrange the leaves and play with the composition before committing to hammering.

3. When you are ready to create the prints, place your cover cloth tightly over the leaves and use a regular hammer to hammer the entire leaf (see page 36); you should be able to see the shape coming through the cloth. Any areas that still appear white should be hammered again.

No two tomato leaves are the same. Look for options with shapes, sizes and structures that you like most.

4   Peeling back the cover cloth should reveal an almost-perfect transfer of the leaf shapes and color onto the fabric.

5   Draw a simple tomato shape on paper, then place your stencil plastic over the top, tape it down, and cut along the outline with an X-ACTO® knife.

6   Tape the stencil in place on your tea towel. Gently rub an orange cosmos flower over the tomato shape of the stencil, making sure not to get under the edges.

7   Take a few remaining tomato leaves and rub them over the stem portion. Repeat several times until you have a good variation of leaves and tomatoes printed on the tea towel.

Pro Tip
When working with a stencil, try not to rub the remaining debris away with your hand. Instead, after you have finished rubbing the flower through the cut design, lift and shake the fabric to remove excess plant matter and to avoid contaminating the surrounding area with unwanted color. You can also wait for the plant material to dry before removing the stencil.

PROJECTS ON PAPER AND WOOD

I have to admit, I tend to enjoy projects on paper even more than fabric. Paper allows a lot more opportunity for creativity. You can easily create mixed-media pieces, scan, and digitize your prints, and the prep time is significantly less than fabric. When you work on paper, you also eliminate the need for "washing" and the everyday wear and tear that fabric experiences. As long as the prints are protected from direct light, they will inherently last longer. Once you master the technique, you will be able to create as you would with any other medium on paper.

One of the misconceptions about printing on paper is that the paper will fall apart when mordanted. While paper is delicate and should be handled with care, it can handle more wear and tear than you might think. All paper can be pretreated using the step-by-step process discussed on pages 48–52. Mordanting paper is an important step if you want beautiful vibrant colors that will last. However, you can certainly skip this step and just start exploring different kinds of paper until you get prints that you enjoy. Exploration will always be key.

Hammered Rubenza cosmos, Japanese indigo leaves, Black Knight scabiosa petals, and Dyer's coreopsis on mordanted mulberry paper.

FLOWERY GIFT TAGS

Flowery gift tags are a sweet and simple project for everyone. Each tag becomes a tiny work of art with endless possibilities. If a flower doesn't print as perfectly as you would like, use it as an opportunity to draw in a few details and add a few of your own designs and a special message onto the tag. I used a fine-tip pen to create leaves and petals on the hammered flowers on my gift tags as an additional embellishment and tied on some raffia for hanging.

There are a number of ways that you can source gift tags. You can make your own from old book pages, scrap paper, or card stock. You can also purchase them from craft stores or online retailers. They come in lots of shapes, sizes, and even colors.

Total hammering time
30 minutes or less

You will need
- Mordanting equipment and materials (see page 48)
- Blank gift tags
- Assorted flowers
- Cover cloth
- Wooden flat surface or cutting board
- Rubber mallet
- Ink pens, watercolors, markers, or colored pencils for decoration
- Raffia, string, or baker's twine for hanging

1. Mordant your gift tags (see pages 48–52) in bulk by allowing them to soak in the solution for 10 minutes, then pulling them out and laying them flat on a towel to dry. Once completely dry, they are ready to be worked with.

2. Put your tags on your cutting board, then place your flowers face down onto your tags and your cover cloth over the top.

I love to create piles of gift tags in the summer months to use throughout the year.

3   Using a rubber mallet, hammer the flowers gently and methodically, making sure you don't hit too hard on the center, and you hammer all the petals. Peel the cloth back to check; if any petals look untouched, repeat the process.

4   Remove the cover cloth and flowers to reveal the prints.

5   Either leave the gift tag as is, or add embellishments with ink pens, watercolors, markers, or colored pencils.

6   Add a 10-in (25-cm) piece of raffia, string, or baker's twine to hang the tag, tying it through the hole punched into the top of the tag.

JAPANESE INDIGO VARIATIONS

Experiment with the plants you have on hand to see what you can create. Leaves, such as mimosa or ferns can imitate the look of a tree without needing the use of a paper punch. Look around your local environment and see what you can find. I like to make these in the summer for use in the winter months. You can draw in details with ink or paint as well.

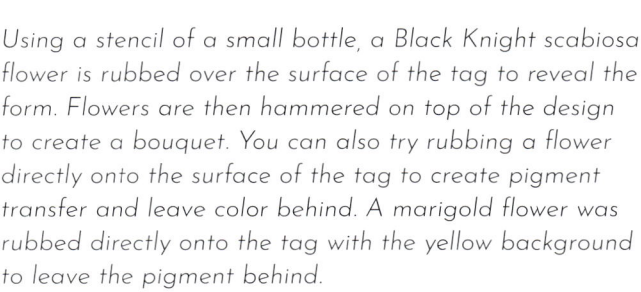

Using a stencil of a small bottle, a Black Knight scabiosa flower is rubbed over the surface of the tag to reveal the form. Flowers are then hammered on top of the design to create a bouquet. You can also try rubbing a flower directly onto the surface of the tag to create pigment transfer and leave color behind. A marigold flower was rubbed directly onto the tag with the yellow background to leave the pigment behind.

Tree shapes are made by using a paper punch on sumac leaves (see page 79). The tree is hammered with the top side of the leaf against the gift tags.

BOTANICAL BOOKMARKS

I absolutely love making hammered flower bookmarks. There is something so magical about using them and preserving the summer on the surface of each one. They can be created in so many ways, with any of the leaves and flowers you have on hand. I used a variety of cosmos and coreopsis, but explore your local environment and see what you can create.

By printing right up to the edges, your bookmark will look like it was cut from a much larger sheet of decorated paper.

Making bookmarks is a multi-step process. You will need to mordant the paper, then create the prints on the bookmarks, and finally seal them and add your tassel. Using a water-based craft glue sealant will give the bookmarks a nice sturdy finish and will protect the prints from wear and tear.

The bookmarks I used for this project measure 6 x 2 in (15 x 5 cm). You can buy premade blank bookmarks at craft supply stores (see page 158) or cut out your own. If possible, use watercolor paper or a heavier-weight card stock that is sturdy enough to support the hole for the tassel. If desired, you can add an eyelet to the hole to give it more strength.

Total hammering time
1 hour per bookmark

You will need
- Mordanting equipment and materials
- Bookmark blanks
- Various flowers
- Wooden flat surface or cutting board
- Rubber mallet
- Cover cloth
- Corner-rounding punch
- Hole punch
- Water-based craft glue sealant
- Foam brush
- String or jute twine
- Eyelets (optional)
- Beads (optional)

1. You can use an internal or external mordant for your paper (see pages 48–52). If you do not mordant your paper, your colors may not be as vibrant as pictured.

2. Put your bookmark on your hammering surface, position a flower face down, and place the cover cloth on top.

3. Hammer gently with the rubber mallet (see page 36), making sure the entire flower has adhered to the paper before removing it. The petals should look flat and translucent.

4. Peel away the petals and continue to create. Don't worry if the flower hangs off the edge of the bookmark, as this will create a more natural look to the finished product.

5. You can also hammer single petals and pieces of flowers and leaves into the negative space so that it feels fuller and more finished.

6   Round the corners of each bookmark using the corner-rounding punch tool, then use the hole punch to make the hole for the string and tassel.

7   Pour a small amount of water-based craft glue sealant onto a piece of paper or an old container lid at your workstation. Apply this with the foam brush to coat the bookmark evenly. Do one side at a time and wait for it to dry fully before moving on. I like to give each side two coats and leave it to dry overnight.

8   Once the bookmark has fully dried and feels sturdy, you can add the eyelet, if desired. Place the eyelet in the hole and hammer flat.

9   Cut a piece of twine or string about 15 in (38 cm) long. Fold in half and push the loop a few inches through the eyelet hole. Grab the other ends of the twine or string and pull them through the loop tightly, making sure not to tug too hard as you don't want to rip the paper.

10 Add beads to the twine or string if you desire, tying a knot so they do not fall off. Unravel the string below the knot to create a tassel.

BOUQUET GREETING CARD

Flower and leaf printing on greeting cards is a fun and easy project for everyone. I like to make extra cards during the growing season to have on hand all year round; after all, flowers aren't just for spring and summer! This project can be altered in a number of ways; you could create a variety of pictures with the flowers such as holiday wreaths, cakes, flower dancers, and more. Let your creativity soar and create beautiful greeting cards from your garden.

Decide on the composition before you start by moving the flowers around on the card, leaving room for writing a greeting or message. I will often take a photo to reference while I am working so that I get the outcome I most desire. I generally don't like the look of most stems when hammered; they tend to be more watery, less pigmented, will often splatter, and do not leave much color. Leaves, on the other hand, are fun to work with so do experiment with different varieties.

You can purchase blank greeting cards at a craft supply store (see page 158) or make your own homemade version with your favorite paper and a bone folder (a tool used to create a crisp fold). I like to purchase blank watercolor paper cards for convenience. They hold excess moisture from the petals and leaves without bleeding and are easy to mordant because of their natural absorption properties. That being said, experiment! Different papers will yield interesting and unique results that you might love.

Total hammering time
30 minutes

You will need
- Mordanting equipment and materials
- Cosmos and coreopsis flowers
- Watercolor paper, or blank watercolor paper cards and a bone folder
- Lightweight rubber mallet
- Cover cloth
- Wooden flat surface or cutting board
- Watercolors, paints, markers, or pens for decoration
- Letter stamps for printing your greeting

1. Follow the steps on pages 48–52 to mordant your greeting cards. They should be completely dry before you begin.

2. Open the greeting card so that the inside is face down and the front of the card is on the right. (The pigment from the botanicals will bleed through and stain the inside of the card if kept folded.)

3. Lay a single flower face down on the center of your card.

Pro Tip

For a clean and precise outcome, work one flower or leaf at a time. If you lay too many flowers down at once, you will run the risk of the plants shifting when you hammer them.

4   Place your cover cloth over the flower and gently hammer the center to "tack" it, without adding too much pressure (see page 36). If you hammer it too hard, the middle will come out messy and blurry. For flowers, hammer each in a clockwise or counter clockwise pattern and be mindful to hit each petal. You should be able to see the shape of the flower through the cloth.

5   Check your progress as you work by gently peeling back the cover cloth to reveal your print. This can help determine if some areas need more hammering than others.

6   Hammer additional flowers clustered together to create the look of a bouquet around your main flower. Add hammered leaves and stems to fill in the negative space, if desired.

7   Add finishing touches by using watercolors, paints, markers, or pens to draw in stems and details. I made my own watercolor by mulling Japanese indigo pigment and watercolor medium to create the beautiful blue paint.

8 Stamp your greeting onto the card. Here I added "happy birthday" using my Japanese indigo watercolor.

9 Hammer a coreopsis onto the back of the envelope for a finishing touch. I did not mordant the envelope to avoid activating the glue seal.

DECOUPAGE FLOWER JOURNAL

There is something about covering a journal or sketchbook with your own artwork that will make it feel not only more personal but also more exciting to use. The journals that I cover with hammered flowers always get the most use. They also make such beautiful, thoughtful gifts that will be cherished by the recipient.

Use flower-adorned paper to decorate surfaces on one-of-a-kind decor pieces, such as journals, holiday ornaments, jewelry dishes, lanterns, and more.

I like to use journals that have a plain kraft paper cover, which is easy to work with and provides a perfect starting surface. They can be brown or white, depending on what is available.

Mulberry paper has a beautiful natural texture that adds to the finished design. Thin and delicate, it may seem too fragile to hammer flowers on to, but I assure you it is not! You can indeed flower pound on to most delicate surfaces as long as you set yourself up for success; you can also use rice paper. Keep in mind that rice paper is somewhat transparent, and the surface of the journal you are working with will contribute to the final design if it is not plain.

I used two mulberry paper sheets, measuring 11 x 8 in (28 x 20 cm), from an online retailer (see page 158), but adapt the size to fit your journal. Mulberry paper is perfect for this technique; combine it with homegrown flowers to decoupage beautiful journals, terracotta pots, seashells, glass ornaments, and so much more.

Total hammering time
2 hours

You will need
- Mordanting equipment and materials (see page 48)
- Mulberry paper: 2 sheets
- Paper towels
- Sponge brush
- Mulberry paper, kraft paper, or thin cloth to place under the project
- Wooden flat surface or cutting board
- Cover cloth
- Rubber mallet
- Flowers: Marigold petals and a variety of both cosmos and coreopsis flowers
- Water-based craft glue sealant
- Journal

1. Use the external mordant method (see pages 48–49) to mordant your paper, reducing the amount of hot water for this recipe from 2 cups (470 ml) to 1 cup (235 ml). This will increase the intensity of the solution and allow more of the mordant to get into the delicate, thin paper. (Keep the quantity of alum to ½ oz (15 g) and soda ash to ⅛ oz (5 g) as per the original recipe.)

Pro Tip
You will only need 2 sheets of mulberry paper for this project, but feel free to mordant other paper you have with the remaining solution. Newspaper and book pages are fun to experiment with!

2. Prepare your workstation, adding a second piece of mulberry paper, kraft paper, or thin cloth below the project to act as a cushion. This will also capture some of the excess moisture and pigment that escape due to the delicate nature of the mulberry paper.

3. Apply the cover cloth and use a rubber mallet to hammer the flowers onto the paper (see page 36). My sheet of paper was larger than one side of the journal, so I only hammered on the portion I needed. Peel back your cover cloth to check that all the flowers have been hammered fully and are attached to the paper.

4. Hammer a second piece in the same way to use for the back of the journal. You will have some transfer to the bottom paper or cloth which can be used for other projects or saved to make tags, gift wrapping, or collage.

5. Lay out marigold petals along the edge of the unused portion of paper to make a simple line design to use for the spine. Hammer these in place. When hammered, marigold petals will leave behind two perfect prints on both pieces of paper.

6. Allow the mulberry paper to fully dry; if you do not wait, the colors will smudge. Lay the paper on the journal before gluing to determine proper placement. I like to have a little extra hang off the edge to wrap around the cover for a more finished look.

7. Once you have decided on placement, it's time to glue. Using your sponge brush, lay a thin coat of water-based craft glue sealant everywhere you want the paper to stick on the cover of the journal.

8. Place the flower paper on the cover of the journal. Once it adheres to the surface, allow it to dry.

Pro Tip
You only get one chance to position your flower paper onto the journal, so be certain you know where you are placing it before you add your glue. Mulberry paper is thin, so it will rip if you try to move it once it has been placed.

9. Once dry, add another layer of water-based craft glue sealant to the top to give the surface durability. Let it dry and repeat with a second coat.

10. Cut the strip of marigold petal prints to use on the spine, glue this down and coat the surface with water-based craft glue sealant. Repeat the same process for the back cover.

WILDFLOWER WOODEN COASTERS

This bright and beautiful set of wildflower coasters will bring a touch of summer to your coffee table.

Believe it or not, you can hammer flowers directly onto wooden surfaces! You can often find precut blank wooden shapes at retail craft stores (see page 158). Items range from coasters to picture frames, ornaments, jewelry trays, and more. It was nearing the end of the growing season when I made these, so I took advantage of the remaining cosmos and coreopsis flowers that were still in bloom in my home garden. I have plans of utilizing this technique on a much larger scale and imagine creating a beautiful hammered flower desktop, or table with a variety of flowers and leaves. If you decide to work on a wooden surface that has been prefinished with paint or stain, it will need to be sanded down before you hammer flowers onto the surface. You want the wood to be as bare as possible when you begin. Be sure to test a small discreet section as well to get a feel for how the flowers and leaves will take to the wood.

I used 4-in (10-cm) square wooden coasters with rounded corners for my project. If you are good at woodwork, these could be easy to make with a variety of wood sold at the hardware store. Adding coaster bumpers as a final step will give the coasters a little elevation so they do not sit flat against the surface of the table when you are finished.

Total hammering time
Approximately 1 hour to make four coasters

You will need
- Mordanting equipment and materials (see page 48)
- Blank wooden coasters x 4
- Flowers: cosmos and coreopsis
- Cover cloth
- Wooden flat surface or cutting board
- Rubber mallet
- High-gloss craft glue sealant
- Foam brush
- Acrylic paint in a color of your choice (optional)
- Adhesive coaster bumpers (optional)
- Hairdryer (optional)

1. Pretreat the surface of your coasters using the external mordant recipe (see pages 48–49) and allow it to fully dry before you start hammering. I applied two coats for these coasters.

2. Use your rubber mallet to hammer the flowers onto the surface (following the instructions on page 36), allowing some to drape off the edge. Repeat for all four coasters.

3   Once you have finished, the coasters should be left to fully dry overnight before adding the high-gloss sealant. You can speed up the drying time using a hairdryer, if desired.

4   Using your foam brush, apply an even layer of the sealant to the front side of each coaster.

5   Leave to cure. The sealant can take up to 4 weeks to fully cure, but it will leave you with a durable, shiny surface.

6   If you would like to, turn the coasters over and paint the back with an acrylic ocher paint.

7   If desired, you can add adhesive coaster bumpers to finish.

WILDFLOWER VARIATIONS

Here hammered flowers adorn a wooden photo frame. After hammering the flowers using the above technique, the final piece was placed in a bath of 1 teaspoon of ferrous sulfate and approximately 1 liter of warm water for around 20 seconds to dull the colors. This gave it a more autumnal feel, which I paired with a vintage photo.

INSPIRATIONAL PIECES

Let's get inspired! The pieces in this section are less dependent on creating a specific look, and are more about exploration and the availability of materials such as flowers, leaves, and other bases. As you have already mastered the techniques, I have not fully illustrated the steps for every piece – that way I could fit more in!

As long as you have a natural fiber and a spark of creativity, you can make all sorts of flower- and leaf-printed products. Items such as vintage textiles, aprons, fabric by the yard, and tote bags should be kept in mind when you're considering a creation.

I often keep a list of items I am interested in creating with in my phone for when I am out and about. If I stop in a thrift store, I can refere nce my list and look for those items while I am there. I try to look for items that really speak to me, and of which I know I will make use. Finding the perfect piece to print on is all part of the fun!

VIOLA AND PANSY TOTE BAG

I live in Zone 5b in the US, where the winters are cold and long, and the last warning of frost can often come in late May. Violas and pansies show up at plant nurseries very early on and are usually one of the first signs that spring is on the way. These prolific bloomers are easy to grow and can be found in less-than-ideal conditions. The more you pick them, the more they seem to thrive.

Surprisingly, violas and pansies are perennial flowers. In my area, they are often treated as an annual flower as they do not survive our winters, but this will be dependent on your climate. I have had success with some varieties returning in pots, and others reseeding themselves throughout the garden. They make a great beginner flower to hammer for children and adults alike and come in a wide range of colors and sizes, which can be fun to explore. It's incredible how perfect a print you can get from these adorable little blooms. You don't need to use as much force as a regular hammer gives, so consider using a lightweight rubber mallet so your flowers do not get too squished and blurred.

Their only setback is that they are not as color- and lightfast as some of the other flowers mentioned in this book, meaning they won't withstand prolonged direct sunlight or hard washings. I chose to work on a tote for this reason; it will get less washings and sun exposure than a garment. Once the prints start to fade, simply add more and continue to build the story of springs and summers past on your project.

LEFT *Violas and Pansies work well on all kinds of fabric and are delicate and easy to hammer.*

TOP RIGHT *When looking for pansies and violas to hammer, gather a variety of different sizes and colors as each one will leave a unique print.*

MIDDLE RIGHT *Tiger Eye violas are especially fun to work with. The delicate line work present on the flower is transferred to the canvas after hammering.*

BOTTOM RIGHT *Pansies are very easy to work with and will provide a perfect little print without much effort.*

1. I scoured the tote (see pages 38-40) and mordanted it with tannin (see pages 41-43) then left to dry fully.

2. I placed the flowers face down on one side of the tote, simply scattering them all around, alternating sizes, and varieties, and keeping equal spacing between the flowers.

3. Using a rubber mallet, I hammered each flower individually to ensure the best results, regularly peeling back my cover cloth to check that the entire flower was hammered and had attached to the fabric.

4. I used an iron on the cotton setting over the top of the prints to help them set.

Pro Tip

It is always good to test your flowers to make sure pigment does not contaminate the other side of your project. You can place a piece of cloth or paper inside of the tote to avoid this; however, due to the relatively low moisture content in these flowers paired with a heavyweight cotton canvas, this may not be necessary.

PANSY AND VIOLA VARIATIONS

Using the same process as the tote, I hammered early-season pansies onto a flour sack tea towel to welcome spring into my home.

This gorgeous vintage dress still had a readable tag. It was 100% cotton, making it a perfect candidate for the printing process.

VINTAGE BOHO DRESS

One of the bigger challenges when working with thrifted or vintage clothing is the fiber content. A lot of older or handmade garments often do not have tags, or their tags are too worn to read, which can be a challenge if you are trying to determine if you have a natural fiber that will accept natural dye. I can often tell by feel, but you want to be certain before you invest time and energy into a project; you don't want to find out the pigment is not bonded to the fiber and will wash right off after the print is finished.

There are simple burn tests you can conduct to help you to distinguish between fiber types, if it is possible to cut a small piece of the fabric in a discreet location of the garment to light. Ask yourself, did the fabric swatch melt or ignite when lit? If it produces a smell of burning paper and grass, it is most likely a plant fiber; if it smells like plastic, it is most likely a synthetic fiber; and if it smells more like burned hair, you most likely have animal fiber.

When working on a large piece such as a dress, there are a few things to consider. It will take a lot of flowers and time to cover it fully. You will want to make sure you work with flowers you have an abundance of, so the colors and shapes are spread consistently throughout the piece. I like to bring large projects outside where I can spread them out. I will often work near the garden so I can pick and choose flowers as needed.

1. I Pretreated the dress in sumac tannin (see page 79) prior to mordanting to give it an all-over pink color. Follow the instructions on mordanting with tannin on pages 41-43.

2. I used a rubber mallet to imprint flowers one by one to all tiers of the dress. I worked on the front of the dress first, varying the flowers, then moved to the back. Here, hundreds of flowers were hammered slowly over a month to create the final piece.

3. Once it was completely finished and the prints had air dried, I ironed the entire piece using the cotton setting to help heat-set the design.

FLORAL FABRIC

If you aren't sure of the design you would like to work on, consider hammering flowers on a piece of plain fabric that can later be transformed into all kinds of projects. From quilting fabric to sewn pieces such as purses and handmade garments, making your own one-of-a-kind flower fabric is always a great idea!

Printing a plain piece of fabric can be a fantastic way to explore flowers and leaves while still creating something useful. If you have a specific project in mind, consider which types of flowers you have on hand or are blooming prolifically in your garden, and which you are certain you will have more of as the season progresses. You do not want to run out of a specific flower or leaf before you have the chance to finish the overall look of the fabric.

I knew this fabric was going to become a pair of sneakers for a collaboration project I was asked to work on. I chose a medium-weight cotton canvas that I purchased by the yard from my local art store. I scoured and pretreated the cotton canvas with tannin (see pages 41–43). I wanted the look to be consistent, as if it had been cut from a much larger piece of fabric. I worked slowly over the course of a month, hammering a little each morning. The piece slowly evolved as my garden did for the season.

The start of the season is a great time to work on larger projects for two reasons. First, the flowers are just starting to bloom, which means many more are on the way. Second, most of the varieties that I speak about are prolific bloomers, so the more you pick and deadhead them, the more they will bloom. By simply working with them you are actually encouraging growth.

Print fabric by the piece or yard so it is ready for embellishing a wealth of projects.

ABOVE LEFT AND RIGHT *For this fabric, I worked with the flowers I had available, spreading each variety out across the entire piece. I used a layering process so that I could evenly distribute each flower variety cohesively. This was important as I wanted both my sneakers to have the same look.*

BELOW *These fabulous floral sneakers were a collaborative project created by I Can Make Shoes, London.*

WILDFLOWER GARDEN APRON

An apron like this is a great project for children and adults alike. I worked a little more intuitively with this piece, as it is simple and requires very little to make. I like that as the seasons go by, I can continue to add to it year after year, imbuing layers of color from my summer gardens.

For this project, I sourced the 100% cotton canvas apron from an online retailer, but plain, basic aprons can also be found at hardware or kitchen supply stores (see page 158). Due to the weight of the cotton canvas, I did not have to worry about the prints bleeding through to the other side. This apron is also only worn one way, so bleed through to the back is not as much of a concern. The end result was super vibrant and made for a nice garden accessory all summer long.

1   I scoured (see pages 38-40) and mordanted my fabric for cotton using a tannin (see pages 41-43) to ensure longevity of color.

2   I then hammered the flowers one at a time, making sure to evenly disperse them across the apron. Starting from left to right, I alternated the size, shape, and color of flowers I had available. I also hammered flowers behind the pockets to add another layer of interest.

I chose cosmos and coreopsis flowers in a variety of colors and sizes to brighten up my apron.

VINTAGE TABLE RUNNER

Vintage table linens can be a great source of inspiration for flower hammering. Napkins, tablecloths, table runners, and doilies can often be found at yard sales and in thrift stores and are inexpensive. Even stained fabric can be perfect for this process as the flowers are excellent for hiding those marks and giving the fabric a new lease of life.

I was given this beautiful eyelet table runner, measuring 32 x 15 in (81 x 38 cm), by a friend. It was her grandmother's and has now become a special and cherished piece to me, adorned with approximately 120 homegrown flowers and leaves. It was mid-summer, and peak growing season when I made this runner. I had an abundance of cosmos and coreopsis flowers available so it was easy to make this piece over a few morning hammering sessions. I try to work evenly and build up the flowers across the width of the fabric when I am hammering to keep a consistent look throughout the project. If you jump around too much you run the risk of having awkward spaces that you may not be able to fill in with the appropriately sized flower. I think part of what makes this runner so beautiful is the close spacing of the flowers. You can achieve this look with any flowers you have on hand as long as you are mindful of the spacing as you work.

This one-of-a-kind table runner is straightforward in its creation.

1. After scouring with my fabric mordant, I started at one end of the runner and hammered the flowers one at a time, to build up the density of the prints.

2. Once the table runner was completely dry, I ironed the whole piece, front and back.

3. I allowed it to cure for 2 weeks before washing it.

FINISHING TOUCHES

Adding embellishments can elevate your flower hammering to the next level. By adding in details you can showcase your drawing style, add more depth with embroidery, and compile scenes that will complement the printed flowers. Embellishments are a way to continue to build creativity into your projects that will make them more interesting and personal. They are also great for adding linework to flowers and leaves that will make the print more defined.

Embellishments can be added in at any time. Embroidery, hand-drawn or painted lines can be added when the cooler days arrive and there are fewer flowers blooming in the garden. Resists can create a space to which you can add a special message when you are ready.

This artwork has been created using a variety of techniques including using stencils, hammering flowers, and transferring pigment by rubbing the flower directly onto the paper.

STENCILS

Stencils allow further exploration of the craft, bringing shape, design, and more imagination to a project. They can be used to create a base layer to add hammered flowers onto. I often use them to create a shape or texture that I think hammered flowers would work well with.

You can create stencils from all sorts of materials including discarded plastic, stencil plastic, paper, iron-on adhesive for fabric, cardboard, and any lightweight material that can be cut with a hobby knife. Stencils can also be purchased in a variety of patterns, shapes, and designs that are precut and ready to go.

These skull socks were created with the use of a skull stencil, then flowers were hammered onto the tops. The purple hue of the skull is from rubbing a Black Knight scabiosa flower over the top of the stencil to macerate the petals and transfer color. The orange color came from Sulfur cosmos, repeating this same technique.

A stencil was also used to create the stems of these flowers branching out from the shirt pocket. I rubbed Japanese indigo leaves over the top of the stencil to make the stems, then the flowers were hammered onto the design.

RESISTS

Resists are used to create an area free of design on your cards, journals, or artwork. I will use a resist if I would like to keep an area blank for adding a favorite word, quote, or sentiment. You could also use the space to add a photo or artwork. This is a great technique for creating personalized journals, greeting cards, and artwork that you can frame.

Resists can be made from cut paper or painter's tape and placed directly onto fabric or paper. Even rubber cement glue can be used as a resist on paper, as you can rub it off once you have finished hammering your flowers.

MAKING A FLOWER FRAME RESIST

You will need
- Paper
- Scissors
- Die-cut machine, paper punch, or painter's tape
- Removable tape
- Greeting card blanks
- Variety of flowers such as cosmos and coreopsis and their leaves
- Rubber mallet
- Wooden flat surface or cutting board
- Cover cloth
- Words or alphabet rubber stamps
- Water-based craft glue sealant

1. Cut out various shapes from paper to lay down on the greeting card blanks. Use a die-cut machine to create an oval shape.

Pro Tip
You could also use painter's tape or removable tape to create the resist shapes. Work in the same way, laying down the tape first, then hammering over the top of it.

2. Use a piece of removable tape to create a loop and attach it to the back of your shape, then stick in place on the card blank. Position the flowers and hammer, following the instructions on page 36.

3. The flowers need to lie partially over the top of the resist shape and the project.

4. Hammer all of your flowers, making sure to go all the way around the resist shape.

5   Pull up the resist and you will be left with a flower frame to use for adding stamped words, calligraphy, or artwork.

6   You can repeat this technique to make squares, diamonds, circles, ovals, triangles, or any shape you can dream up.

7   You might wish to stamp a piece of cardstock with various words, then cut those words out and add them to the center of your design. You could also stamp, write, or paint directly inside the frame.

8   Secure in place using a little water-based craft glue sealant below and over the top of the words.

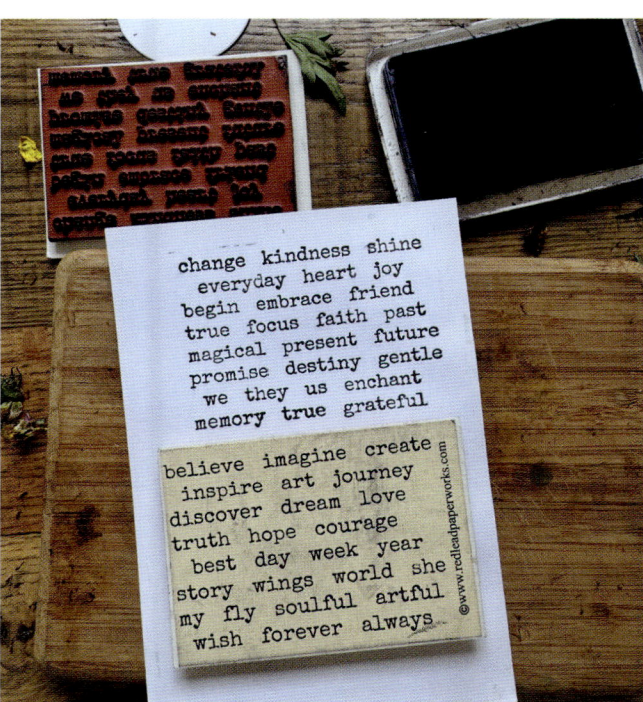

ARTWORK

Wall art can be just about anything that you can dream up – that is the fun of this beautiful art form. So, dive in and create anything you can think of using petals and leaves. If you create a print that does not look how you wanted, consider drawing or painting in lines that will transform the pigment into something more recognizable, like a bug or animal. The process can be advanced by hammering the individual petals and leaves into a complete form, resembling a person, an animal, a mandala, or any other creative object that comes to mind. Allow the inherently painterly and unique feel of each print to inspire your artwork.

Sometimes hammered prints have less-than-desirable results, and when that happens you can often study the prints to see what else they can become. You may have noticed the addition of paint, ink, watercolor, pencil, or marker details on some of the earlier projects. You can add as many or as few details as you would like to finish the artwork. These can really enhance a design and bring it to life.

I enjoy creating dresses and fashion designs from the flowers and seeing how the personality of the figure develops organically as I continue to layer the hammered petals and leaves. I will sometimes create without a true plan and intuitively hammer each petal and leaf with care. Other times, I will look for inspiration from a recent runway event or theme, and design with that idea in mind.

It is also great to experiment with different papers. I like using hot press watercolor paper as it has a smooth flat finish that is perfect for hammering flowers and using ink with a paintbrush. Cold press papers will have a "tooth" or texture that will add an element that you may like.

LEFT I first hammered a cluster of flowers onto paper, then I painted the bottom portion of a woman's face using homemade Japanese indigo watercolor paint.

ABOVE I love to make floral arrangements by drawing or painting a bottle, vase, or vessel, then hammering flowers coming out of the top.

RIGHT Here, single petals are hammered to represent the wings and bodies of insects. Ink is then added over the top to create the line work for the bugs.

As an artist, I don't think we need much to be creative or inspired. Here, single marigold petals were hammered onto the paper one at a time, then I inked lines with a micron ink pen to form flower people. The shape of the petals inspired the personalities of the flower people.

I added line work with a pen to bring this figure to life. The end result is a whimsical one-of-a-kind creation born from hammered flowers and leaves.

Coleus and Smoke bush (cotinus) leaves, together with coreopsis and marigold flowers, make up the dress here.

RIGHT *I first used painter's tape to create a border all around the artwork – a nice way to add a finished look to a piece. Flowers were then hammered and ink added to create a scene. I then rubbed marigold and scabiosa petals directly onto the paper to create a background color.*

DIGITIZING YOUR WORK

Paper prints in particular are really easy to scan or photograph, allowing you the opportunity to experiment even further as you can transform the color, scale, and pattern of the art. These works can then be elevated into prints, products, and other small batch-printed items.

For this process, I typically use Adobe Photoshop. However, there are a number of "art to product" websites that allow you to upload a photo of your finished artwork and apply it to customizable products.

I recommend taking a photo of your work on a white background in bright sunlight. You want the best possible image when working with digitally printed items. You can then crop and edit your photo as required on your smart phone and upload it to one of the sites. It is so much fun to see your hammered flower and leaf artwork become prints, patterns, and products.

ABOVE *A notebook digitally printed with soy-based inks from a design made with hammered flowers.*

TOP RIGHT *Thank you card digitally printed with soy-based ink.*

BOTTOM RIGHT *"Anthophile" Print made from hammered flowers and digitally designed.*

EMBROIDERY

Embroidery can really enhance a design — you can even embroider paper! Study your hammered flower print and think about how you can really make it pop. What details can you accentuate?

Perhaps the center could use a few French knots, or the leaf print would look nice with a fern stitch? I love what a little string and a few creative stitches can do to elevate a piece.

ABOVE *Look closely! French knots are added to embellish the centers of the hammered flower design.*

ABOVE *The addition of these details is always aided by an embroidery hoop to hold the fabric taut.*

PAPER PUNCHES

Paper punches add another layer of creativity to a project. They are available in craft stores, online retailers, or marketplaces, and even thrift stores (see page 158) and come in a variety of shapes for all seasons and holidays. You can also get them in the shape of a gift tag, or as geometric shapes that you can use as paper resists.

You can use paper punches in two different ways, both of which are effective in adding imagery to your piece:

1. Use the punch on the actual leaf or flower petal, as you would a piece of paper. Once punched, you can hammer the shape directly onto the surface of your project.
2. Use the punch on a piece of recycled plastic, card stock, or cardboard to create a stencil. You can then rub petals and leaves through to create the image on your paper or fabric.

Try to avoid bulky leaves when working with a paper punch – thicker or waxier leaves will be hard to cut through. Staghorn or Smooth sumac, Japanese indigo, birch, oak, and Black walnut leaves are all good choices; you can even use some larger flower petals.

Some leaves will slide easily into the punch slot; others will be more difficult. If you aren't able to get a clean punch, place the leaf in between a sheet of parchment or wax paper. The paper will make it easy to get a clean cut every time – after all, punches work best with paper!

Pro Tip
When it becomes difficult to get a clean cut, sharpen old punches by punching through a sheet of aluminum foil multiple times.

RIGHT A tree shape is punched and hammered onto a small pouch.

OPPOSITE A vintage butterfly paper punch is used to create shapes from Staghorn sumac leaves to hammer onto fabric.

148

PRACTICE PAGES

Photocopy these three pattern pages to practice your technique – each design was purposely left unfinished so that you can finish the artwork, and I have provided a photo of my finished version of the designs below to give you inspiration. You can recreate the designs shown in a number of ways: by laying a lightweight paper or tracing paper over the page; photographing/scanning the design and printing it on thicker paper; or you can photocopy each page and trace it onto your own paper or fabric. Lastly, you can also experiment with working right on the page and see what you can create.

To transfer onto paper, place the printed or photocopied page against a light source (a sunny window works well for this), with your project paper taped over the top of the artwork. This process will also work well with thinner fabrics. Next, add to the design. Hammer flowers and leaves or rub flowers directly onto the paper to explore color and pigment transfer. Get creative, enjoy the process and see what you can discover in the world around you.

RIGHT Hand holding flowers. This design – screen-printed onto a cotton t-shirt – is a tribute to the summer garden. Pansies, cosmos, coreopsis, and Black Knight scabiosa flowers were hammered on to the design. Additionally, coleus, Japanese indigo, and random floral foliage was added.

FAR LEFT Peace wreath. This design features a peace sign with a vine wrapping around it and was screen-printed onto a long-sleeve t-shirt. I then added several varieties of cosmos and coreopsis flowers to the design.

LEFT On the windowsill. This artwork was created on watercolor paper. The finished piece uses hammered coreopsis and cosmos flowers. The background color was produced by rubbing flower petals from marigolds onto the paper. The colors inside the bottles were made from Black Knight scabiosa and Blacknight Hollyhock flowers. Treat the page like a coloring book, with the garden as your art supplies!

HAND HOLDING FLOWERS

PEACE WREATH

ON THE WINDOWSILL

GLOSSARY

A **Alum acetate:** A purified fine mordant powder used in natural dye to bond pigment to fiber.

Animal fibers: Fiber derived from animals, such as silk, wool, alpaca, and angora.

Anthocyanin: A blue/red/purple pigment found in plants, which is sensitive to light and pH.

C **Cellulose fibers:** Fiber derived from plants, such as cotton, bamboo, hemp, flax, and ramie.

Curing: The amount of time given after mordanting to give your fiber increased durability and fastness so that it can better withstand the elements.

D **Dye bath:** Created by simmering plant matter in water to remove pigment to dye fiber with.

Dye pot: A stainless-steel pot used for mordanting your fabric or to prepare a dye bath or mordant.

F **Fastness:** The ability of fabric to endure light, washing, rubbing, and wear and tear without bleeding or fading. The capacity to retain color without changing.

Ferrous sulfate: A blueish-green crystalized iron compound used in natural dyeing to mordant and/or modify the color of natural dyes.

I **Iron water:** A solution made by adding equal parts of vinegar and water plus rusty items to create a solution for mordanting or modifying.

M **Mordant:** Typically, a metal salt that will adhere to a fiber so that natural dyes can bond to it. This will increase over wash and lightfastness.

N **Natural dyes:** Pigment from plants, insects, animals, minerals, and other places found in nature used to change the color of fabric and paper.

Natural fibers: Any fiber that is derived from nature.

P **Paper punch:** A tool used to cut a shape from paper or (in this book) plant matter.

pH: A scale from 0 to 14 used to identify how acidic or basic a solution is.

pH neutral: In this book, used to refer to a substance that will not alter the color of a natural dye due to acidity or alkalinity, such as laundry detergent.

Potassium alum sulfate: referred to as "alum," a metal salt used to mordant fabric and paper.

R **Regular hammer:** A tool that consists of a weighted head and a claw or ball. Most commonly used to drive nails into wood.

Rubber mallet: A tool with a rubber head. Often significantly lighter than a regular hammer, it will deliver a softer impact to the object being struck.

S **Scour(ing):** The removal of manufacturing chemicals, waxes, dirt, and debris that finds its way onto your fabric.

Stencil: A thin sheet of plastic, paper, or metal used to lay over a surface. Pigment can then be applied through the cut-out shapes.

Stencil plastic: Plastic that can be sourced from discarded containers, packaging, or purchased sheets to carve into for making patterns and shapes on fabric and paper.

Synthetic fiber: Man-made fibers that contain chemicals including fossil fuels and petroleum products, such as nylon, polyester, and spandex.

T **Tataki-zomé:** A Japanese term used to define the art of hammering leaves and flowers onto fabric to retain color and prints. Translates to "hammering dye."

Texture hammer: A tool with interchangeable heads that will leave a pattern or texture on the item it has struck.

W **Weight of fiber (WOF):** The measurement of the weight of your fabric, preferably after it has been dried and scoured.

RESOURCES

I have used all of the below resources over the years to assist in my development of this craft and overall understanding of the natural dye process. Through workshops, books, online resources, and perusing local farms, I have been able to build my skills and knowledge. I am grateful to all those that have come before me to offer their passion, insight, and inspiration. As a result, they have given me the opportunity to discover these processes to hammer my own path.

I always try to source as much as I can from my local region first, but when that is not possible, I use the below retailers.

WEBSITES

EDUCATION AND NATURAL DYE RESOURCES

Canada
MAIWA
maiwa.com/collections/natural-dyes
For natural dye supplies, blanks, education.

Israel
Irit Dulman
iritdulman.com
Natural dye education.

UK
Botanical Inks
botanicalinks.com
Natural dye supplies and education.

Wild Colours
wildcolours.co.uk
Dyestuff for natural dye projects.

US
Botanical Colors
Botanicalcolors.com
For natural dye supplies, blanks, education.

BLANK PRODUCTS FOR DYEING

Canada
MAIWA
maiwa.com/collections/blanks
Blank textiles for natural dye.

UK
Cloth House London
clothhouse.com
Fabric for natural dye.

George Weil
georgeweil.com
For art and craft supplies.

Greenfibres
greenfibres.com
Blank textiles for natural dye.

US
Botanical Colors
Botanicalcolors.com
For natural dye supplies, blanks, education.

Dharma Trading Co.
dharmatrading.com
For natural dye supplies and blank textiles for dyeing.

PAPER PRODUCTS

UK
Eco-craft
eco-craft.co.uk
Eco-friendly stationery and paper products.

US
Paper Mart
papermart.com
For paper and pouches.

Red Lead Paperworks
www.redleadpaperworks.com
For stamps and stencils.

SEEDS AND STARTS

UK
Chiltern Seeds
chilternseeds.co.uk

Special Plants Nursery
specialplants.net

Wild Colours
wildcolours.co.uk

US
American Meadows
americanmeadows.com

Farmer Bailey
farmerbailey.com

Grand Prismatic Seed
grandprismaticseed.com

Siskiyou Seeds
siskiyouseeds.com

BOOKS

Behan, Babs, *Botanical Inks: Plant-to-print Dyes, Techniques and Projects*, Quadrille Publishing Ltd, London, 2018

Cardon, Dominique, *Natural Dyes: Sources, Tradition, Technology and Science*, Archetype Publications Ltd, London, 2007

Dean, Jenny, *Wild Color: The Complete Guide to Making and Using Natural Dyes*, Potter Craft, London, 2010

Flint, India, *Eco Colour: Botanical Dyes for Beautiful Textiles*, Murdoch Books, Sydney, 2021